The Dalton Gang and Their Family Ties

by
Nancy Ohnick

with contributions by:
Nancy Samuelson • Bill Phillips,
Glen Feldman • Roger Meyers

Published by
OHNICK ENTERPRISES
Meade, Kansas

The Dalton Gang and Their Family Ties
Third Edition

PO Box 969 • Meade, Kansas 67864
www.prairiebooks.com
Manufactured in the U.S.A.

ISBN 0-9746222-1-4

From the Editor

This book is dedicated to Dalton descendants everywhere who search for their family ties.

The little house in this photo was built in 1887, by J. N. Whipple for his bride, Eva Dalton. The house still stands on the corner of Pearlette and Green St. in Meade, Kansas. Legend has it that Eva Dalton Whipple helped her outlaw brothers and their gang and provided an easy access to her home through a tunnel from the barn to the house where they could enter undetected by the neighbors and the law. The original tunnel, which was an old rain wash covered with boards and dirt, was reconstructed in 1940 to allow safe passage for the many visitors who come to the site each year.

For those of us who live in Meade, Kansas, it is our tie to the way things were in those wild and woolly days of the Old West of which we were a part. We invite you to visit Eva's little house... a honeymoon cottage... an outlaw hideout.

The Preservation of an Outlaw Hideout

In the southern part of Meade, Kansas, four blocks south of highway 54, still stands the two-room house that was first occupied by Mr. and Mrs. J.N. Whipple. Eva Dalton, sister of the infamous outlaws, married J.N. Whipple October 15, 1887, at which time they moved into the newly constructed house Whipple had built for his bride. The house was on the outskirts of town in those days; the landscape dropped sharply from the house to a streambed to the south where water occasionally flowed into Crooked Creek to the east. A sharp bluff to the south of the streambed formed a canyon of sorts, later dubbed, "Gallop Away Canyon." Taking advantage of the landscape, Whipple built his house half underground with one exposed wall and a door leading from the basement to the south. Their barn also was half sheltered by the earth in the hill below.

Eva Dalton came to Meade shortly after the town was established in 1885. She was engaged in a millinery business with Florence Dorland, who later married R.A. Harper, an early-day Meade County rancher.

Whipple operated a mercantile store on the northwest corner of the square. Fairly successful as a businessman, he was reported to have been a good poker player, often holding games at the Whipple home.

The Dalton brothers were reportedly seen several times in Meade before a price was set on their heads, but their sister was never heard to mention their names after they became famous.

The Whipples left Meade by early 1892, and their property was sold under foreclosure. Soon after, the H.G. Marshall family moved into the house. The new occupants discovered a tunnel from the house to the barn. Inside the house the mouth of the tunnel was hidden by a small closet beneath the stairway leading to the two-room basement of the place. The tunnel was constructed by placing beams of wood across a deep rain wash which were then covered with earth. It was barely large enough for a man to walk through in a stooped position. From the house the tunnel led into a small feed room in the barn, which hid the tunnel entrance.

One of the Marshall daughters, Mrs. Roy Talbott, often told the story that several times horseback riders came up the canyon to the barn; placed their hoses in the barn and came on into the house through the tunnel. When the surprised riders learned that another family occupied the house, other than the Whipples, they immediately fled back through the tunnel, mounted their horses and galloped away.

Legend has it that many of the old-timers of Meade were very friendly with the Dalton Gang and thus the gang never raided the Meade banks or committed any overt acts in this vicinity. Old timers were always tight lipped about the notorious brothers.

In 1934, the Wayne Settle family was living in the house. At that time an old man came through Meade from Ohio on

his way to California. He drove down to the house and visited a half hour with the Settle family. He told them of the days when he was with the gang and of the tunnel. The Settle family did not know of its existence. The entrance under the stairway had been rocked up and the basement given a coat of plaster over the natural rock walls. However, the old fellow showed them where the rocked-up entrance was and examination showed that the rocked-up entrance was recessed four inches deeper than the wall.

When the Dalton Gang Hideout was developed as a tourist attraction in 1940, Frank Fuhr, former editor of the Meade Globe Press, recalled that many times he had watched riders come up the canyon and into the barn. He stated that he never saw the riders come out of the barn and go to into the house and he suspected there was a tunnel. Later he learned of its existence, but he did not dare mention it back in the eighties. Fuhr lived across the canyon south and west of the Whipple property and became so intrigued with the activity at the Whipple home he purchased a spyglass to watch the comings and goings of the gang.

In 1940, many older residents remembered the secret tunnel and the youngsters of the nineties remembered playing in it. This editor interviewed Mrs. Byron Fisher who lived across the street from the property during her childhood. She said she and her brother played with the children who lived in the Whipple house. She remembers playing in what was left of the tunnel from the barn entrance, she doesn't remember too much about it, but can remember that they called it the "tunnel."

In the 1940's NYA crews constructed the the 95-foot long tunnel that connects the house to the barn built into the hill below. The original tunnel was a deep rain wash covered with boards and earth.

The Whipple house belonged to many different people over the years. Henry F. Danks owned the house from 1898 to 1911, this photo shows a well-kept home with fine architectural detail.

Photo courtesy of Larry MeyerS

The photo above shows the house as it appeared in 1914, the man in the photo is Mr. Cord Kruse.

This editor received a letter in 1988, from Mr. Clyde W. Blackburn, respected treasure hunter and historian from Leoti, Kansas. We had discussed finding proof of the tunnel at an earlier date. Mr. Blackburn wrote: "I really don't think I can add too much as that was over fifty years ago and I wasn't at all that interested in history at that time. I was surprised at your remark that there was no proof the tunnel was actually used by the Daltons. Certainly that much work wasn't done for the fun of it. If my father were still around I am sure he could have added some proof as he was a true history buff and spent a lot of time in the Meade and Clark County area over the years. He was a good friend of Lon Ford, the colorful sheriff of Clark County, and was with him on several excursions. I have tried to call on my memory as to what he told me about the house, tunnel, and barn but it is so hazy I can't seem to put it together. I do know he was well acquainted with the lady who lived in the house at the time and had apparently been there many years before. This is no doubt the reason I was given free run of the tunnel and all the relics, which were stacked and hanging in the barn. It was a rather eerie trip as I walked down the tunnel with the dirt walls, which as I remember, were supported somewhat haphazardly with occasional boards. For the life of me, I can't remember where I got the information, but somewhere I gained the fact that on three different occasions the Daltons visited Meade and that on at least one of them did use the tunnel to make their escape."

An Invitation to the World

The Dalton Gang Hideout as a tourist attraction found its beginnings in 1940. Walter and Ruth Dingess were operating a café in Englewood, Kansas, and looking for a place to open a museum to house their growing collection of artifacts.

Walter was, in fact, checking with the Big Well in Greensburg the day Joe Ross and J.W. Cooper went to his cafe to approach him with the idea of coming to Meade. The two left word for the Dingess' to come to a Chamber of Commerce meeting and present their ideas, which they did—the rest is history.

Mr. Ross wasn't even aware at the time of the historical significance of the little house at the corner of Pearlette and Green Street;

The Dalton Gang Hideout as it appeared in the early 1940's.

From the Meade Globe Press in 1940: "This is the Dalton Gang Hideout as it will be restored by the City of Meade. The artist, Harry Wells, has indicated in his drawing how the tunnel led from the house to the barn, where it ended in a small feed room. Old timers state that the drawing is correct in every detail except that the old well was nearer the house."

his father brought it to his attention and it turned out to be the perfect solution for the City of Meade and Walter and Ruth Dingess.

The house was acquired by the Chamber of Commerce by means of a trade for another house, and in May, 1940, the Dingess family moved in. The sketch by Harry Wells illustrates the plans they had to rebuild the tunnel and barn.

Walter, Ruth, and their teenage daughter lived in the little Whipple house for five years. They lived upstairs while selling their souvenirs from the basement.

Much of the landscaping and improvements to the Dalton Hideout were accomplished by use of WPA labor. These crews built the rock retaining walls and NYA crews reconstructed the tunnel and the barn. Rock for the projects was quarried from the Clark Ranch east of Meade. The park was completed two years later in March, 1942.

In 1951 Mr. Dingess built Dad's Country Store, the 10'x12' building with a roofed porch just south of the wishing well. In 1988, the Chamber of Commerce added a building to house handicap-accessible restrooms to the east of the Whipple house.

Except for the cottonwood trees that have grown to gigantic proportions in the little park south of the barn, and these recent additions, the Hideout looks much the same as it did in it's beginning in 1942.

Walter Dingess retired in 1956, and turned the gift shop and souvenir business over to Ruth. She operated the Hideout until 1970. The Chamber of Commerce operated the Hideout until the property was deeded over to the Meade County Historical Society in 1995.

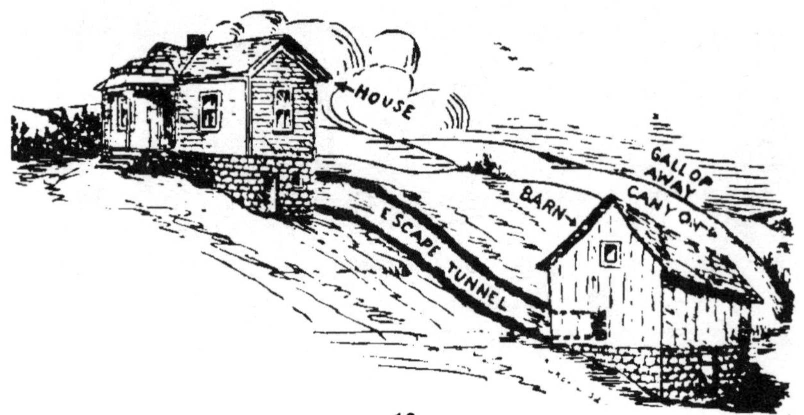

The Dalton Gang Hideout Museum offers a grand collection of prairie artifacts such as this unique two-headed calf.

Several animals native to Southwest Kansas are mounted and posed as they would appear in the wild, such as the bobcat in the photo below.

A large assortment of horse bits on loan from a private collector is one of the more unique collections on display in the museum.

Branding Irons, saddles, and other cowboy gear are on display in the loft of the barn, as well as other artifacts of frontier life.

Information about the Dalton Family and the desperadoes who rode with them is on display in the loft of the barn.

The large chandelier in the center of the loft is made with a wheel from one of the first street sprinklers in Meade. From this are suspended seven old-time coal oil lanterns.

The basement of the Whipple house is furnished like the kitchen of the 1880's.

In this tiny room is where the opening to the tunnel is.

The upstairs in the Whipple home is furnished as it would have been when Eva lived there. A sewing machine, vital to a milliner, graces the living room.

The Wishing Well in the Hideout yard, as well as all the other stone work was done by WPA crews in the early 1940's.

This covered wagon made the trip to all the big round-ups of the area in the 1880's. It was the property of F.M. Steele, a frontier photographer who left a valuable record of early-day farming and ranching.

EVA & JOHN

by Nancy Ohnick

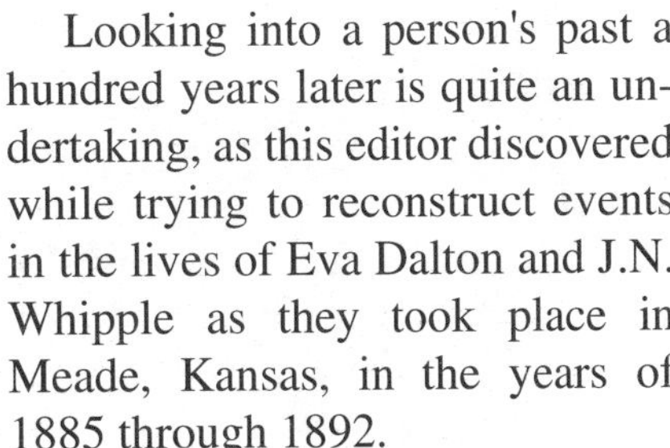

Looking into a person's past a hundred years later is quite an undertaking, as this editor discovered while trying to reconstruct events in the lives of Eva Dalton and J.N. Whipple as they took place in Meade, Kansas, in the years of 1885 through 1892.

I have been through all the local newspapers of the day (there were three of them in Meade Center at the time), through many records in the Register of Deeds' Office and the Treasurer's Office in the Meade County Court House, as well as all the history books I could find. The following is my conclusion supported by all the above.

It seems that J.N. Whipple and R.A. Harper had been friends for a long time. History tells us that Mr. Harper came to Meade County as early as 1884, when he came through on a cattle drive from Texas and decided to homestead here. I have no background on Mr. Whipple, but his ads for Whipple's Headquarters, "The Buffalo Store," start showing up in the local papers when they began in 1885. Some think he was the first merchant in Meade Center (as Meade was called in the early days). One local newspaper says he was formerly of Wellington, Kansas.

I mention them both because their lives seem to be intertwined throughout my story. They married best friends and seemed to remain close through the years I traced them.

John Whipple was a merchant. He had a mercantile store on the northwest corner of the square in Meade. From his ads we see he sold fancy groceries, fine clothing, boots, shoes and gents furnishings, wholesale and retail. It was named the "Buffalo Store" and a sign was displayed in the front of his building with a picture of a buffalo.

A bachelor in his mid-thirties, John Whipple was a well-respected businessman. He made the local "City News" any time he went away on business, had a mishap, or was taken ill. I first find John in this column when he served on the refreshment committee for the grand opening of the New Opera House. One article recommended him as good material for City Council in an upcoming election. He must have been friends with the newspaper editors as they referred to him as "Johnny Whipple" and "Whip" on several occasions.

We don't know when Eva Dalton and her friend Florence Dorland came to town. They were said to have come from Chetopa, Kansas, and that

This street scene of early-day Meade was referred to as "north of the square." The building on the far left would have been where Whipple's store was located in 1885.

they opened a millinery store in Meade. Chetopa is a small town just east of Coffeyville; history tells us that Eva's parents lived near Coffeyville at this time.

The early papers liked to list the businesses that were in the "boom" town of Meade at that time, and in the February 25, 1886, issue only one millinery store is listed. Other newspaper tidbits tell us that this store on the southwest corner of the square belonged to Mrs. M.A. Williams. In the May 7, 1886, issue of the Meade County Globe we see two millinery stores listed. It stands to reason, if indeed Eva and Florence had a store, it may have gone in sometime between February and May of 1886.

Florence is easy to trace in the papers. Her sister was Mrs. George DeCow (pronounced de-coo) who lived on a ranch south of Meade. We find news of Florence visiting and having callers at the ranch often. George, also a businessman, put in a billiard parlor (of good reputation) early in 1886. One paper lists, "George DeCow, one of the old settlers of '78 is a candidate for Sheriff." All in all, a popular bunch.

In my search of the papers I ran across a real estate transfer of some Meade County farmland from a John Dalton. Investigation showed that John C. Dalton and wife Mary A. Dalton homesteaded 160 acres of land about 5 miles straight south of Plains, Kansas, applying for their homestead December 23, 1886. They sold this land

April 1, 1887. In the "City News" of the Meade County Globe, May 1886, we find mention of a Mr. J. Dalton visiting the editor who described him as "a reliable citizen of Rainbelt." Rainbelt was a small, unplatted community northwest of Meade at the time. One can't help but wonder if this was an uncle of Eva Dalton and that would perhaps provide a connection for her to come to Meade. History shows that her father had a brother named John, but we know nothing about him.

Other Daltons found to have homesteaded in Meade County are Jehn (could be Jehu) and Martha who homesteaded in 1890, turned right around and mortgaged the property and then abandoned it—it was repossessed in 1891. (This homestead was just three miles from John C. Dalton's land.) Robert A. and Rosa E. Dalton did the same thing at the same time on another homestead, this one being just two miles northwest of Rainbelt. It was a popular "scam" of the day to homestead a property, stay until papers were issued, then mortgage the property and take off with the proceeds.

I searched and searched for ads for a millinery store in the old papers, but never found one. A few businesses owned by women were briefly mentioned but the feeling was they were not taken all that seriously. Eva really doesn't show up in the records until she married Whipple on October 25, 1887. It is the same year Florence Dorland married R.A. Harper.

On September 15, 1887, J.N. Whipple bought the property on which the Hideout now stands for $400. He first bought a lot one block west in March but this one must have been a more suitable site on which to build.

When John and Eva were married, all three Meade papers carried the story of their wedding. My favorite came from the Meade County Press-Democrat as follows: "The home of Mr. and Mrs. Geo. DeCow, who live four miles south of town, was the meeting place Tuesday evening of a number of the friends of Mr. J.N. Whipple, one of our most prominent business men, and Miss Eva Dalton, a young lady of rare beauty and intelligence. The occasion was the solemnizing of the marriage by Judge Hudson of Mr. Whipple and Miss Dalton. The bride and groom were supported by Mr. and Mrs. Robt. Harper. The ladies were dressed in wine-colored silks trimmed with lace, the gentlemen wore the customary dress suit. After congratulations of the numerous friends the entire company repaired to the dining room where a magnificent feast was waiting, the result of the united efforts of Mesdames Harper, DeCow and Black. The presents were numerous and elegant. It is with pleasure that the editor of the Press-Democrat announces the marriage of these friends and we join with all in wishing them a happy and prosperous life."

The Meade Globe Republican reports: "A guest informs us that the groom appeared at his best and that the bride was a perfect picture of loveliness and beauty. Those who are acquainted with her know her to be an excellent lady, attractive and accomplished. The groom has undoubtedly secured a prize. Mr. Whipple is one of our leading merchants, sociable and financially prepared to fill all the demands of the new relation.

Well, if Whipple was financially prepared it wasn't evident when, not even a month later on November 16, 1887, his property was deeded over to Guy C. Scott for $400. We learn from the old papers that Scott was a money-lender who set up office in Meade that same year. Also on that day Whipple sold 160 acres of farmland south of Missler, Kansas, (about six miles west of Meade) to his good friend, R.A. Harper.

November is also the last time we see Whipple's Headquarters advertised in any of the local papers. Had he gone out of business so soon?

On January 18, 1888, a Quit Claim Deed is recorded showing the property on which their home stood rewarded back to Eva Whipple for the sum of $450. Guy C. Scott made some pretty good interest there! On January 20th J.N. sold his other lot west of their property for $100.

In April, 1888, an ad for Hassett's New Store lists its location as "Whipple's old stand." J.N. most assuredly went out of business. Had the beautiful Miss Dalton been the beginning of the end for ol' Whip? Did his marriage to Eva create a notable difference in his life style?

All the deeds after their marriage appear in Eva's name. Eva Whipple and husband or at least with Eva's name first. Eva was the name on the tax rolls. This would seem a little odd in that day, or even today for that matter.

On July 3, 1888, Eva bought 160 acres of land on the same section J.N. had owned land before (the land he sold to Harper). She bought 160 acres for $700 and turned around on September 26, and sold it for $1900. She must have had a head for business! 160 acres was the amount of a homestead, which is probably why so many land purchases were in that amount.

According to the September 21 edition of the Meade County Globe, their daughter, Maude Whipple, was born September 14, 1888, so all this activity was taking place while Eva was "great with child."

The tax rolls indicate that Eva paid her taxes faithfully through 1888. On July 1, 1889, they mortgaged their property to the Central Kansas Loan & Investment Company for $350. Taxes were billed to Eva but not paid in the years of 1889, 1890, 1891 and in January of 1892 they missed their first mortgage interest payment resulting in a repossession of their property in the amount of $58.75 + costs. The mortgage on file in the Meade Court House has coupons attached that show that the Whipples made their interest payments up to January 1892. When the sheriff tried to deliver the summons for the foreclosure on February 16, he noted that John N. Whipple and Eva Whipple were not in his county and could not be served, "am informed that the defendants reside in Oklahoma," was his recorded comment.

On November 19, 1892, the property was sold at a sheriff's sale to Sumner W. Pierce for $50.

We can't prove that the Whipples stayed in Meade until 1892. All we know is that they paid their mortgage payments but not their taxes, and we do not know where they went from here. It has been recorded in the journals of U.S. Marshals as close as Dodge City that Eva Dalton Whipple "bore watching," and that they kept an eye on her because of her activities connected with her brothers. It would stand to reason that the Whipples would keep a low profile if they were indeed connected with the gang.

One can't help but feel that J.N. Whipple may have had to pay dearly for the prize of the beautiful Eva Dalton, and then again, the life they led may have suited him well.

The Harpers remained prominent citizens of the area, R.A. became a very successful rancher and a banker in later years, helping to establish the Fowler State Bank in 1908.

We find Eva mentioned when the gang met their demise in Coffeyville on October 5, 1982. She traveled to Coffeyville with her mother and brothers, Bill and Ben, to take care of Emmett Dalton who was severely wounded in the attempted raid on two banks on the same day. Emmett eventually recovered from the twenty bullet holes that riddled his body and as he was being shipped off to Independence, Kansas, to stand trial, he sent the last of his possessions, a scarf pin, to his mother who "languished in Kingfisher."

The Whipples reportedly lived in different towns in Oklahoma. Eva once owned property in Purcell, and a 1902 City Directory from El Reno lists her as a dressmaker at 616 N. Evans. They eventually settled in Siloam Springs, Arkansas, where they operated a restaurant in the 1920's. After John died, Eva moved to Kingfisher, Oklahoma, to live with her sister, Leona. John lived to the age of 81, Eva to the age of 72. Together it seems, until John's death in 1932.

A census taken near El Reno, Territory of Oklahoma, in 1900 tells us that they had another child, Glenn B. born in April, 1894. Eva's obituary lists only a granddaughter as her survivor at the time of her death.

And to this Union a Daughter is Born...

The picture above right is of Maud Whipple, the daughter of John and Eva. It was discovered among the relics in the Hideout Museum. On the back of the picture, Mr. Dingess, originator of the museum, wrote: "Maud Whipple, Niece of the Dalton boys, made about 1890, property of Mrs. H.M. Coon, Meade, Kansas." There is also the stamp of the photographer: J.W. Mosser, Meade Center, Ks.

Mrs. Dingess remembered quite well when Mrs. Coon brought them the photo. They had just opened the museum. Mrs. Coon, then Eva Wiley, had been a neighbor of the Whipples and as a young girl stayed with them to help with the baby. Eva Wiley would have been eleven or twelve at the time.

In the Meade County History Book, Eva Coon recalls the time in her "Pioneer Story": *"We also lived in the south part of town near the Dalton Hide Out which was the home of Mrs. Eva Whipple, a sister of the Dalton boys, and I stayed with her at night for a week, while Mr. Whipple was away. They had a baby girl named Maud and her picture is now at the Hideout. Eva Dalton and Florence Dorland came from Chetopa, Kansas, and opened a millinery store before their marriages to J.N. Whipple and R.A. Harper, both from Texas. Mr. Whipple had a grocery store and Mr. Harper was a rancher."*

A copy of the twelfth census of the United States taken near the City of El Reno, Canadian County, Territory of Oklahoma, on June

18, 1900, lists Maud B. Whipple, born February, 1888, in Kansas. We have tried to locate a birth certificate in the Meade County records without success.

Eva Coon left Mrs. Dingess with the impression that the Whipples did not leave Meade until after the Dalton Gang became well known for their lawless activities. People here knew their connection to the Dalton family and asked too many questions; the Whipples left to avoid the shame brought on by the outlaw brothers.

The picture above is the only photograph this editor has ever seen of Eva Dalton Whipple. It was taken in their restaurant in Siloam Springs, Arkansas, in the 1920's.

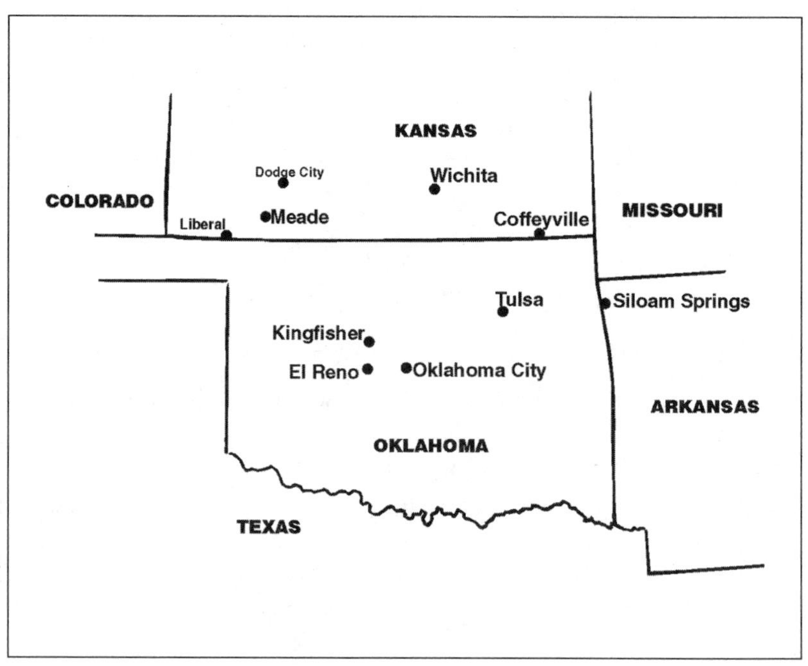

The Dalton Family

by Nancy Samuelson

A lot has been written about the Dalton Gang, and much of what has been written is nonsense or pure fiction. Early writers invented "facts" and these "facts" have been copied and repeated by later writers. Some writers are still inventing new stories about the Dalton Gang family. Much of the literature in books and Western mag-

Nancy B. Samuelson, Lt. Col. USAF. Ret.

Nancy Samuelson was born November 12, 1940, in Dent Co. Missouri. She is the daughter of Raymond and Rosa Dalton McDonough. She has a Bachelor of Arts degree from Harris Teacher's College, St. Louis, Missouri and a Master of Business Administration from Syracuse University.

Nancy served in the United States Air Force from 1964-1984. She served in a variety of management and command positions in the logistics career fields for about fifteen years; then as an Assistant Professor of Aerospace Studies in the Air Force ROTC (Reserve Officer Training Corps) program at the University of Connecticut. She is also the graduate of a number of professional military schools. Military awards and decorations include the Bronze Star, the Meritorious Service Medal and Outstanding Supply Officer of the Year. Overseas tours of duty were in England and Thailand.

Nancy is married to Dr. Reid R. Samuelson (PhD Electrical Engineering) also a retired Air Force Lt. Col. The Samuelsons live in a 200 year old house in rural Connecticut.

Since retirement, Nancy keeps busy with research, writing and gardening activities. Research and writing projects focus primarily on women in the military, western history and genealogy. Her articles and book reviews had appeared in Air University Review, Armed Forces and Society, Minerva, Quarterly Report On Women And The Military, The Herb Quarterly and in a number of genealogical publications.

Her interest in the Dalton Gang began when she started researching her own Dalton family line. Both families came from the same general area of Virginia, but so far no common ancestor has been found.

Nancy Samuelson has published a book, The Dalton Gang Story, that contains a much more in-depth look at the Dalton family as well as copies of all the materials she used to document the facts she presented here. It is recommended reading for Dalton family members who want genealogical information. Shooting Star Press, PO Box , Eastford, CT 06242.

azines such as *Real West, True West*, etc. is extremely inaccurate. *The Dalton Gang* by Harold Preece is a very readable book about the Daltons but it contains a lot of incorrect information.

The best book to date about the Daltons is *Dalton Gang Days* by Frank F. Latta. Latta repeatedly interviewed Emmett Dalton, the brother who survived the Coffeyville, Kansas, bank robbery attempt; Littleton Dalton, an older brother of the outlaws; and numerous lawmen who were involved in attempting to bring the Daltons to justice.

Latta had to wait until after Emmett's death to publish his book because Emmett refused to allow anything to be published that disagreed with his two books, *When The Daltons Rode* and *Beyond The Law*. Emmett's books contain a lot of fiction and they do not always agree with each other. *West Of Hell's Fringe* by Glenn Shirley is a well-researched and documented book and contains a lot of material on the Daltons.[1]

The Dalton Gang consisted of Robert, Gratton and Emmett Dalton, and various other men who rode with them when they robbed trains. The entire outlaw career of the gang lasted just about two years. The first robbery attempt was in Alila, California , in February, 1891, and the gang's activities ceased in October, 1892, when they attempted to hold up two banks at the same time in Coffeyville, Kansas. Robert, Gratton and two other gang members were killed in the Coffeyville raid. Emmett was badly injured; he received about twenty bullet wounds. He was sentenced to life in prison but was pardoned after serving fourteen and a half years.

Robert, Gratton and an older brother, Frank, had all served as U.S. deputy marshals out of Fort Smith, Arkansas, before the younger brothers turned to crime. Emmett had also served as a posseman with his brothers. Frank Dalton was killed while trying to arrest whiskey runners in the Indian Territory. After his death the other three brothers were accused of stealing horses. The ex-police Daltons then left the Oklahoma Territory and joined the older brothers in California and shortly after turned to robbing trains.

Bill Dalton was the fourth of the Daltons to turn outlaw. He was not a member of the Dalton Gang, but after the Coffeyville raid he joined the Bill Doolin Gang. After several robberies with the Doolin

Gang, Bill and three other men robbed the bank in Longview, Texas. Bill was killed June 8, 1894, when he was surrounded by U. S. marshals near Ardmore, Indian Territory (Oklahoma).

There are several train and bank robberies that were clearly the work of the Dalton and Doolin Gangs. However, the Daltons were frequently accused of other crimes they obviously did not commit. Some authors have also connected the Daltons with the James and Younger Gang. The Daltons and the Youngers were cousins, but there has been no relationship discovered between the Daltons and the James boys. The James-Younger band started their outlaw activities after the Civil War. The James and Younger brothers had all served in guerilla units during the war with the notorious Quantrill. After the war they turned to outlaw activities. The Daltons were all too young to serve during the war and did not begin their activities until after the James-Younger Gang was out of business. The Younger brothers were captured in September, 1876, after an attempt to rob a bank in Northfield, Minnesota. Jesse James was killed April 3, 1882, by Bob Ford, a member of his own gang. Frank James surrendered to the Governor of Missouri shortly after Jesse's death.

To further confuse the Dalton - James connections, a man named J. Frank Dalton, supposedly about age 97, turned up in Lawton, Oklahoma, in 1948, claiming he was the real Jesse James. He claimed another outlaw, Charlie Bigelow, had been killed and passed off as Jesse. Dalton convinced many people of his claim and went on the lecture circuit. J. Frank Dalton died in Granbury, Texas, in 1951, and was buried under the name Jesse James. Still another Dalton, Kit Dalton, author of a completely fictitious book, *Under The Black Flag*, claimed connections with both the Jesse James and Sam Bass outlaw gangs. Kit died in Memphis, Tennessee, in 1920. Both J. Frank and Kit claimed to be related to the Dalton Gang. No proof of any relationship between J. Frank or Kit Dalton and the Dalton Gang has yet been uncovered.

The parents of the Dalton Gang were James Lewis Dalton and Adeline Lee Younger.

James Lewis Dalton was born in Montgomery Co. Kentucky, February 16, 1826. He died in Montgomery Co. Kansas, July 16,

1890, from a sudden attack of cholera morbis. Lewis served in the Mexican War as a fifer in Company I, 2nd Kentucky Infantry. He joined the Army at Mount Sterling, Kentucky, May 25, 1846, and mustered out in New Orleans, Louisiana, June 9, 1847. Lewis married Adeline Lee Younger March 12, 1851, in Jackson Co. Missouri. She was born there in 1836, and died in Kingfisher, Oklahoma, at age 92. She was the daughter of Charles Younger and Parmelia Dorcus Wilson. She was a half sister to Henry Washington Younger, father of the Younger brothers.[2]

Many authors have made much ado about Lewis Dalton's love of horses and horse racing. There are many claims that he kept his family poor with his horse racing and trading activities. There are numerous claims that he and Adeline did not get along in later years and even stories that she divorced him. Lewis certainly did travel all over with his horses and the family was never financially well off. However, Lewis and Adeline started for Oklahoma in a covered wagon in 1890. Lewis became ill on the way and died. He is buried in the Robbins Cemetery near Dearing, Kansas. Adeline collected a widow's pension after Lewis died so it is clear there was no divorce.

Lewis certainly did love his ponies but there were also other circumstances that contributed to the tribulations of the Daltons. The Civil War undoubtedly had a large influence on the family. The Daltons started out in Jackson Co. Missouri in 1851. According to Littleton Dalton, the family was near Denver, Colorado, in 1860, and then near Lawrence, Kansas, in 1861. Later they moved to Liberty, Missouri, to get out of the fighting zone. Census records show they were in Cass Co. Missouri in 1870, and in Bates Co. Missouri in 1880. All of these western Missouri counties suffered greatly during the Civil War and it is almost certain that some of the moves the family made were the result of the war. This is the area that was frequently raided by the Kansas Redlegs and Jayhawkers. This is also the area where Quantrill's men dug in and fought back at the Kansas forces. The infamous Quantrill raid on Lawrence, Kansas, took place on August 21, 1863.

General Thomas Ewing, Jr. was in command of a large area of this border area where the guerrilla warfare was centered. He believed the Union Missouri Militia was too soft in dealing with the pro-southern people in Missouri. He began arresting and confining wives, mothers, and sisters of some of the most notorious members of Quantrill's band. On August 14, 1863, the prison in Kansas City where these women were held collapsed killing four girls and seriously hurting others. Some of these injured women were Younger relatives of Adeline Dalton. Then on August 18, 1863, Ewing issued Order No.10 which stated that children and women who were heads of families and who willfully engaged in helping of guerrillas were to be sent south out of the state of Missouri.[3]

Quantrill's men retaliated by raiding the town of Lawrence, Kansas. Then Ewing issued his infamous Order No. 11 on August 25, 1863. This order reads in part as follows: *"All persons living in Jackson, Cass, and Bates counties, Missouri, and in that part of Vernon included in this district, except those living within one mile of the limits of Independence, Hickman Mills, Pleasant Hill, and north of Brush Creek and west of the Big Blue are hereby ordered to remove herewith. Those who, within that time, establish their loyalty to the satisfaction of the commanding officer of the military station nearest their present place of residence will receive from him certificates stating the fact of their loyalty, and the names of the witnesses by whom it can be shown. All who receive such certificates will be permitted to remove to any part of the State of Kansas, except the counties on the eastern border of the State. All others shall remove out of this district. Officers commanding companies and detachments serving in the counties named will see that this paragraph is promptly obeyed.[4]*

Order 11 made the three counties of western Missouri a wasteland for the remainder of the war. Almost the entire population of the area was evacuated and this undoubtedly included the Dalton family. In addition, Adeline's brother, Henry Washington Younger, was murdered by Kansas Jayhawkers on July 20, 1862. Later the Younger home was burned and the family turned out in winter weather. Mary Josephine Josie" Younger, sister to Cole, John and Jim, married John Jarrett also one of Quantrill's men. There is a story that they were victims of an ambush after the war. Their house was set on fire and John and Josie perished in the fire. Their two children were rescued from the fire.[5]

The wartime experiences of the Dalton and Younger families must have had some influence on the younger Dalton children. No one has ever suggested that the trials of the war years influenced the Dalton boys to turn to crime but these incidents must have left their marks somewhere along the way.

There has been considerable confusion about the parents of Lewis Dalton, father of the Dalton Gang. Several genealogies have been published showing Lewis to be the son of James Lewis Dalton, Sr. This is not correct as can be shown by the records of the James Lewis Dalton, Sr. family which will follow. This idea probably stems, at least in part, from Charles Younger's will, which bequeaths "to Adeline L. Dalton, wife of Lewis Dalton, Jr., the tract of land containing two hundred and ten acres on which said Dalton and wife now live in Cass Co. near Harrisonville." The Jr. was probably used in this case to distinguish the younger Lewis from his uncle Lewis Dalton who also lived in the vicinity.

Littleton said his grandmother was Nancy Dalton. He said his father and all of his father's family were born in the neighborhood of Lobergrub, Kentucky. Littleton was uncertain about the exact spelling and location of Lobergrub. Further research has revealed the neighborhood was Lulbegrud, and is located in Montgomery Co. Kentucky. The name was established in 1770 when Daniel Boone and a party of hunters and explorers made camp in the southwest section of what is now Montgomery Co. The party was attacked by a band of Indians and after a brief skirmish, the Indians were driven away. Before the attack the Boone party had been listening to tales from Swift's *Gulliver's Travels*. The account that night was of Gulliver's experiences with the Lulbegruds , mythical inhabitants of Glumdelick. After the Indians had been driven off the remark was made, "We've driven off the Lulbegruds." The campsite was named Lulbegrud and a small stream in the area still carries the name today. In addition, in 1793, the Lulbegrud United Baptist Church of Jesus Christ was established in the area.[6]

Benjamin and Lewis Dalton, both born in Virginia, came to the Montgomery Co. Kentucky area around 1812. Ben appears on the Estill Co. tax lists from May, 1812, through 1814. He then appears on Montgomery Co. tax lists from 1816 through 1829. Lewis Dalton appears on a Montgomery Co. tax list in 1821 and remained in this county for another 20 years.

Henry Rabourn settled in Montgomery by 1803, and purchased land on Lulbegrud Creek three miles nearly due south of Mt. Sterling. On October 25, 1823, Ben Dalton bought land adjoining the lands of Henry Rabourn. Ben and Lewis married daughters of Henry Rabourn. Ben married Nancy Rabourn April 16, 1815. Ben died in Decatur County, Indiana, January 15, 1835. Lewis Dalton married Matilda Rabourn February 20,1821, in Montgomery Co. Henry Rabourn's will names both Nancy Dalton and Matilda Dalton and identifies them as his daughters.[7]

Benjamin Dalton served in the War of 1812 in Captain Silvanus Massie's Company of Infantry, 2nd Regiment Kentucky Militia. Nancy Dalton filed a claim for a widow's pension in Belton, Missouri, on May 3, 1879. She was 86 years old at the time. Appearing with Nancy to file her pension claim were Lewis Dalton, age 79, and Henry M. Dalton age 57.[8]

In the 1860 census Nancy Dalton, age 47, born in Kentucky, is shown as living with the family of William Chism in Jackson Co. Missouri. Her age is probably wrong. This is almost certainly the widow of Benjamin Dalton and William Chism is Nancy's son-in-law. The census further shows William Chism, age 24, farmer born Illinois; Agnes Chism, 35, born Kentucky, and John B. Chism,1, born Missouri. Marriage records of Jackson Co. Missouri show William Chism married Agnes Dalton on May 16, 1856.

Littleton Dalton mentions two of his father's sisters and indicates that his father had other brothers and sisters. One sister is Tillie Louis, who was probably living in Missouri when Adeline and Lewis were. Littleton said Aunt Tillie got a wood stove the same time his mother did. Tillie was so disgusted with the wood stove she went back to cooking on the fireplace. Another sister was Nancy Emollient who married Robert Noel. The Noels married in Kentucky and went to California in the 1850's. Both lived until past 80. Henry Coleman Dalton, Littleton's brother, was named for brothers of both his mother and father; Coleman Younger and a brother of the father, named Henry, who died in Kentucky.

The James Lewis Dalton, Sr. in Jackson Co. Missouri was the uncle of Lewis Dalton who was the father of the Dalton Gang. This is very clear from evidence in census data, the warranty deed of October 2, 1880, filed on the estate of Lewis Dalton, and the Bible records of Henry Milton Dalton, son of Lewis and Matilda Dalton. The Lewis and Matilda Dalton family came to Jackson Co. Missouri in 1841. There were five children in this family. Henry Milton Dalton married Nancy Martha Johnson. Nancy married first James Helms and second Isaac Andrews. Armilda (Ormilda) married Samuel H. Luttrell. James Lewis Dalton married Margaret _____. David G. Dalton married Georgie Hannen.

James Lewis Dalton died June 22, 1879, age 80 and Matilda died Feburary 19, 1879, age 76. They are buried in the Dalton or Luttrell Cemetery in Jackson Co. Missouri. [9]

This author believes Ben and James Lewis Dalton, Sr. are brothers but no proof of this has been found. The 1810 census for Pittsylvania Co. Virginia, shows Ben Sr., Ben R. and Lewis Dalton. The 1820 census for this county shows only Ben Dalton. One Ben and Lewis have left that county by 1820.

The Dalton Children

Several sources say that Lewis and Adeline Dalton were the parents of fifteen children. Littleton says there were ten boys and five girls. Emmett in *Beyond The Law,* published 1918, lists fifteen children as follows: "Ben, now a farmer in Oklahoma; Cole, now living in New Mexico; Louis, who is dead; Littleton, still a ranchman in California; Lelia, who is dead; Frank, who was killed while serving as a United States marshal; Gratton, who was killed in the Coffeyville, Kansas, raid; William , a stock raiser in California, now dead; Eva, alive; Robert, who was also killed in Coffeyville; myself; Leona, also alive; Nammie(sic), dead; and finally the twins Simon and Adeline, of whom Simon is still alive." [10]

1. **Charles Benjamin Dalton** The oldest son was undoubtedly named for both grandfathers, Charles Younger and Benjamin Dalton. Ben was born February 24, 1852, probably in Cass Co. Missouri. He died in the state hospital in Ft. Supply, Oklahoma, March

Charles Benjamin Dalton

16, 1936. He owned land and farmed for a number of years in Kingfisher Co. Oklahoma. He was described as slow and at one time as looking older than his mother. The cause of death is listed as apoplexy with contributory cause of cerebral arteriosclerosis. He never married. Several authors have listed this man as two different people: as Ben and as Charles. Census records and the death certificate make it very clear there is only one individual named Charles Benjamin Dalton.[11]

2. **Henry Coleman Dalton,** born November 26, 1853. Littleton says he was named for brothers of both the mother and father. Cole, as he was called by the family, died in Des Moines, New Mexico, on February 28, 1920. Cause of death was listed as tubercular pleurisy, contributory cause tuberculosis. Cole lived and worked in California for a number of years. During the last ten years or so of his life he lived in New Mexico. He had gone to that state hoping the climate would improve his health. Cole never married.[12]

3. **Louis Kossuth Dalton**,born July, 1855, died 1862. Littleton says he was named for a famous Austrian patriot, and that he died at the age of six or seven. (Lajos Kossuth was a Hungarian patriot who fought, unsuccessfully, for Hungary's independence from Austria).

4. **Bea Elizabeth Dalton.** There is controversy among various Dalton researchers about this Dalton sister. There are claims that another sister died as a child and this woman who married Thomas Louis Phillips is not a daughter of Lewis and Adeline Dalton. This author has not been able to find absolute proof one way on the other. The evidence will be presented and the readers can judge for themselves.

According to the Phillips family, Bea Elizabeth Dalton was born March 14, 1856, and died December 28, 1894. The family had a death certificate (delayed filing) created for Bea Elizabeth a few years ago and also had the death certificate of her son Jack Phillips, amended. Jack Phillip's death certificate originally gave his mother's maiden name as Harrison and this was amended to read Dalton. The fact that a delayed filing death certificate was created and another death certificate was amended has led several researchers to question the validity of these documents.

The death certificate of another of Bea Elizabeth's sons does give the mother's maiden name as Dalton and the Phillips family bible has Bea Elizabeth's birthday, marriage date, and names of parents recorded in it. Further, some members of the Phillips family have the name Dalton as a middle name. A John Phillips served as a pall bearer for Simon Dalton's funeral and the inscription "John Phillips, Guthrie OT" appears on the side of Nancy Dalton Clute's tombstone. John Phillips was a son of Bea Elizabeth.

According to the Phillips family Bea Elizabeth married first a man named Harrison. She had a little girl during this marriage and the child was killed in a grassfire near her home. Mr. Harrison died and Bea Elizabeth was working in a hotel in Brownsville, Texas, when she met and married Tom Phillips, a Texas Ranger. The family later settled near Tussey, Oklahoma. Tom Phillips died in May of 1930. There were five children born to this couple. John William born 1882, died 1963, Alford Lee born 1884, died 1931, Robert Louis born 1888, died 1953, and twins Jack Jesse born 1891, died 1974 and Pearl Katie born 1891, died 1920. Several grandchildren and great-grandchildren still live in Oklahoma. Bea Elizabeth does not appear on any of the census records that have been found for the Dalton family, but no 1860 census record for them has ever been located. The family was probably moving around in the Kansas Territory and was missed in that census. Bea could easily have been gone from home by the 1870 census. Emmett does list a sister Lelia in *Beyond The Law*. The Daltons were fond of nicknames and Lelia could easily have been a nickname for Bea Elizabeth. There is no evidence found by this author to identify anyone else as the sister Lelia.[13]

Littleton Lee Dalton

5. **Littleton Lee Dalton** born October 2, 1857. Littleton was named for an uncle, Littleton Younger, who moved from Missouri to Oregon. Littleton lived in California and worked on ranches most of his life. He never married and he died in the Yolo Co. California hospital January 2, 1942. Immediate cause of death was bronchi-pneumonia. He also suffered from senility and generalized arteriosclerosis. He was buried in Woodland Cemetery, Woodland, California. [14]

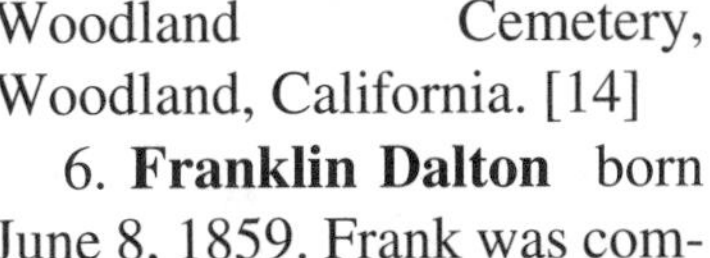

6. **Franklin Dalton** born June 8, 1859. Frank was commissioned U. S. deputy marshal at Fort Smith, Arkansas, in 1884, and was killed near Fort Smith on November 27, 1887, while trying to arrest whiskey runners. It is not known for sure if Frank was married or not. Some of the dime novels have him married to women named either Naomi or Julia. No marriage record has been found and newspaper articles about Frank's death do not agree on his marital status. Frank was a widely respected law enforcement officer and his death was a real blow to his family and friends.[15]

Franklin Dalton

7. **Gratton Hanley Dalton "Grat"** born 1861. According to Littleton, Grat was named for old Kentucky neighbors who were also probably relatives. Grat never mar-

Gratton Hanley Dalton

ried. He died at Coffeyville, Kansas, October 5, 1892. Before turning to crime Grat had served as a U. S. deputy marshal for the Fort Smith court and had once been wounded in performance of his duties. In 1931, when Emmett returned to Coffeyville for a visit he said, "Poor Grat. Here he sleeps, an aimless, discontented boy who grew into a fierce fighting man."[16]

Mug shot of Grat Dalton when he was arrested in California.

8. **Mason Frakes Dalton "Bill"** born 1863. Several published books and articles give Bill's name as William Marion. However, he is shown on several census records as Mason Frakes and Littleton said he was named for an old southern farmer his father stayed with for awhile in Missouri. Bill died June 8, 1894, in Elk, Indian Territory, while trying to escape from U.S. marshals. His body was taken back to California for burial by his wife. He was first buried in the yard of his father-in-law's home, but when the family sold the house Bill Dalton's body was supposedly reburied in the cemetery in Turlock, California. Bill was shot while running away from the officers who

were trying to arrest him. The story that he was shot in the back while playing with his daughter was an invention of Emmett.

Mason Frakes "Bill" Dalton at a young age.

Bill was a well-respected farmer and local politician in California before his brothers staged their first attempted train robbery. However, the often-repeated stories that he had served in the California legislature or even that he had run for Governor of California are without foundation. Bill was arrested and tried for the Alila robbery but was acquitted. The accusations against Bill may have caused him to turn bitter toward the law and probably influenced him to turn to criminal activities later on.

Bill Dalton the way he looked about the time he was killed.

Bill returned to Oklahoma a year or so before the Coffeyville robbery. After his brothers were killed at Coffeyville he vigorously protested the manner in which the law had treated the bodies of his brothers and settled the estates of Bob and Grat. Shortly thereafter he joined Bill Doolin, a previous member of the Dalton Gang. The Doolin Gang committed several robberies, and Bill had probably split from the Doolin Gang and branched out on his own shortly before he was killed. Bill, Jim Wallace, and two Knight brothers robbed the bank in Longview,

Texas, on May 23, 1894. Shortly after this robbery Bill was surrounded and killed by U. S. marshals.

There are reports that Bill was married to or at least fathered a child by Mary Hughes in Oklahoma. No proof of a marriage has been found but the descendants of a William Harmon Dalton identify themselves as descendants of Bill Dalton. William Harmon had two daughters (twins). Thelma Mires (granddaughter) had three daughters. This author remains very skeptical of the Mary Hughes story.

Bill married Jane Bliven in California and had two children by this marriage. These children were Charles Coleman "Chub" and Gracie. Chub married Emma Turner and they had six children. Charles Coleman died May 4, 1967, in Lodi, California. Emma died January 24, 1969, in Lodi. Some of their children and grandchildren still live in California.

Gracie was crippled from an injury suffered in a fall. Gracie married Leslie Rhodes of Eldridge, California, and she had one son. Gracie died in 1948 and her husband, Leslie, died in 1959.

Jane Bliven Dalton married Joseph "Bob" Adams after Bill was killed. She and Adams had one daughter, Orva. Orva married Lloyd O. Beam. He died in October, 1938, and Orva died in September of 1970. [17]

9. **Eva Mae Dalton** born January 25, 1867. Eva taught school for awhile. She married J. N. Whipple of Meade, Kansas on October 25, 1887. She is known to have worked as a milliner and a dressmaker. She also ran a restaurant in Siloam Springs, Arkansas. After her husband's death in 1932, she made her home with her sister Leona in Kingfisher, Oklahoma, until her death on January 28, 1939. She was survived by a granddaughter Mrs. W. D. Meadows of Houston, Texas.[18]

Eva Mae Dalton in her early fifties.

The 1900 census for El Reno, Canadian Co., Oklahoma, show John, born 1851, Eva born 1867, Maud B. daughter born 1888 and Glenn B. son born 1894.

10. **Robert Rennick Dalton** born 1869. Littleton says Bob was named for a chaplain with General Jo Shelby of Civil War fame. Bob died on October 5, 1892, at Coffeyville. He never married. There are various tales about a girlfriend of Bob who tapped telegraph lines to obtain information about trains with gold shipments. One story has her dying of cancer just before the Coffeyville raid. Various sources identify her as Florence Quick, Mr. Mundy, Tom King, Eugenia Moore, etc. These tales appear to have sprung from Emmett's fertile imagination.

Robert Rennick Dalton

There is also an often-repeated tale about how Bob Dalton shot Charlie Montgomery in the back because Montgomery had taken up with Bob's girlfriend Minnie Johnson. Minnie is reportedly Bob's cousin. This author has not been able to uncover a single shred of evidence that any girl, cousin or otherwise, named Minnie Johnson ever had any connection with Bob Dalton. Bob did shoot and kill a man named Charlie Montgomery. Montgomery was wanted for horse theft, impersonating a law officer and several other offenses. Bob was one officer in a three-man posse sent to arrest Montgomery. Montgomery fired on the posse twice. Then Bob shot and killed him. [19]

Bob Dalton and Unidentified woman in 1889.

11. **Emmett Dalton** born May 3,1871. According to Littleton, Emmett was named for an Irish orator, Robert Emmett. This has been cited as evidence of Irish ancestry by some authors, but there is no proof of any Irish connections for this family that has been found so far. (Robert Emmett was an Irish rebel who led an attempted insurrection against the British. He was convicted of treason and hanged). Emmett was badly injured at the Coffeyville raid and was sentenced to life imprisonment. He was pardoned after serving almost 15 years in the Kansas State Prison. After his release from prison he married Julia Johnson Lewis of Bartlesville, Oklahoma, September 1, 1908. Emmett makes much in his books of Julia's waiting faithfully for him while he was in prison. However, Julia married at least twice and possibly three times before she married Emmett. She married Robert Gilstrap, and had one daughter, Jennie Gilstrap, born November 17,1887. Gilstrap was killed by Frank Lenno in December, 1889, and in the early 1900s Julia married Robert Earnest Lewis. Lewis was killed in a shootout with U.S. deputy marshals in his saloon in Bartlesville in 1907.

Mug shots of Emmett Dalton arrested for bank robbery and murder in 1892.

There are several stories that Julia was married to Albert Whiteturkey before she married Bob Gilstrap. No documentation for this marriage has been found. One story has Julia married to Whiteturkey for eight years before she married Gilstrap. This is ridiculous as Julia was only sixteen years old when she married Gilstrap. Julia's daughter, Jennie, married twice and had four children, two boys and two girls. Julia cared for a foster child for a number of years. She took in this child while Earnest Lewis was still living and this boy lived with her and Emmett for awhile after their marriage. The boy's name was Roy Reynolds. Roy was adopted several years later by people named Johnson. These Johnsons were not related to Julia. Roy went by the name of Roy Reynolds Johnson and his wife was named Grace. This couple had at least three children and possibly four. This family was last known to be living in Houston, Texas.

Julia died in Fresno, California, on May 20, 1943. The cause of death was cardiac failure due to a ruptured appendix. Julia had married again after Emmett's death. Her last husband was John R. Johnson of Los Angeles.

After Emmett was pardoned he lived for a short while in Oklahoma, then moved to California. There he became a building contractor and real estate agent. He wrote two books about his outlaw days *Beyond The Law* and *When The Daltons Rode.* Several motion pictures were made about the Daltons and Emmet acted, and assisted in production of several of these films. Emmett was financially very successful for several years but there are reasons to believe he had lost most of his money before he died.

Emmett got religion before he died and he was baptized in Aimee Semple McPherson's "Angelus Temple" in August of 1936. Emmett suffered from the effects of a serious gunshot wound in one arm all of his life. He had surgery and various treatments for this wound throughout his life but the wound never healed. Two or three years before his death Emmett had a stroke and he remained in poor health after this. Emmett died July 13, 1937, from a second stroke. According to his death certificate he also suffered from hypertension and diabetes. Emmett made much of his childhood romance with Julia Johnson in both his books and in interviews with newspa-

Emmett Dalton and his wife, Julia, at their home in California.

Emmett Dalton

per reporters. There is, however, little or no evidence to support the story of young love. It is most likely that Emmett first met Julia after he was released from prison in 1907.

Both Emmett and Julia were cremated and Emmett's remains are buried in an unmarked grave in the family plot in Kingfisher, Oklahoma. Julia is buried in a cemetery in Dewey, Oklahoma. Her grave has a simple marker that says, "Julia J. Dalton 1870-1943".[20]

12. **Leona Randolph Dalton** born July 17, 1875. Leona never married and cared for her mother and her nephew for much of her life. She worked as a seamstress and dressmaker for several years. She did very fine work and a beautiful wedding dress she made is on display at the Chisholm Trail Museum in Kingfisher, Oklahoma. She was a well respected and much loved member of her community. Leona was born with a cleft palate and as a result had a speech impediment. She died in the Hukills Rest Home in Kingfisher of acute bronchial pneumonia on April 18, 1964. She had been bedfast for some time before her death. Due to some sort of mix-up both Leona's death certificate and her obituary give the name of

Leona Dalton

her father as William Dalton. This information is incorrect as there is no doubt that she was the child of Lewis and Adeline Dalton. [21]

13. **Nancy May Dalton "Nannie"** born March 11, 1876. Nancy died in Kingfisher on December 27,1901. She died of lockjaw as the result of a smallpox vaccination. Nancy is buried in the Kingfisher Cemetery where the inscription on her tombstone was written by her mother. It reads: "Beautiful spirit freed from all pain/ ours the loss, thine the eternal gain."

Nancy married Charles M. Clute January 22, 1896, in Kingfisher. Before moving to Oklahoma, Charles had been engaged in the hardware business in Chicago for about ten years. Nancy had one son, Roy Clute. Roy was raised by Leona after Nancy's death. Roy Marselus Clute was born August 11, 1897, and died April 12, 1978, in Tulsa, Oklahoma. Roy and his wife operated motels for a number of years. Roy had one daughter. [22]

14 and 15. **Hanna Adeline Dalton and Simon Noel Dalton** born July 6, 1878. Hanna Adeline died at birth or shortly after. Many authors have claimed Simon died at age 14. This is not true. Simon Noel enlisted in the Army November 14, 1899, and was discharged December 15, 1902. He served in the Philippines for most of his enlistment. He was discharged in California and later returned to Oklahoma. Simon married Minnie (Mamie) McDaniel on July 30, 1910, at Nowata, Oklahoma. She must have died before he did as his death certificate lists him as a widower. It is known that Minnie had a son before she married Simon but no further information has been found about her or the child.

Simon had a reputation as a never-do-well and he was not overly fond of work. However, he is known to have worked in the oilfields as a construction worker. He applied for a disability pension from the Army in September,1925, but the application was rejected because he had only minor medical problems. According to the application he needed to wear glasses to read, had some teeth that needed to be pulled, and had hemorrhoids. Simon was badly injured when the car he was driving was hit by a train in June, 1928. He died in the University Hospital, Oklahoma City, on September 13, 1928, from pneumonia and from fractures and internal injuries suffered in the accident.[23]

Notes

1. Frank Latta, DALTON GANG DAYS [book] (Santa Cruz, Bear State Books, 1976) All statements throughout this article attributed to Littleton Dalton are from DALTON GANG DAYS or from unpublished statements made to Latta by Littleton. Latta papers are owned by Brewer's Historical Consultants in Exeter, California. Author reviewed these papers in December of 1988.
2. Military Records of Lewis Dalton. "Mrs. Adeline Dalton ", KINGFISHER FREE PRESS, January 29, 1925. Marley Brant, THE FAMILIES OF CHARLES LEE AND HENRY WASHINGTON YOUNGER, [book] (Burbank, California, 1986) p. 9-10.
3. Donald R. Hale, WE RODE WITH QUANTRILL [book] (1982) p. 50.
4. H.H. Crittenden, THE CRITTENDEN MEMOIRS[book] (New York, G. P. Putnam's Sons, 1936) p. 349.
5. Marly Brant, op. cit. p. 16.
6. Unpublished History of Lulbegrub Church. Courtesy Mt. Sterling, Ky. Public Library.
7. Estill and Montgomery Counties, Kentucky tax and marriage records. Nancy Dalton's pension application, filed Belton, Missouri, May 3, 1879. Henry Rabourn's will, proved May 1839, Montgomery Co. Kentucky.
8. Military record of Benjamin Dalton. Pension application of Nancy Dalton.
9. Census records, Montgomery Co. Ky. 1830, 1840. Jackson Co. Mo. 1850, 1860, 1870. Warranty Deed October 2, 1880 filed Jackson co. Mo. January 22, 1881. Mary Ann Van Zant Bell. DALTON DATA VOL I [booklet] "Dalton Bible Records. (Spokane, Wa. 1985.) p. 2-3.
10. Emmett Dalton, BEYOND THE LAW, reprint REAL WEST, August, 1971. p. 44.
11. Death certificate of Charles B. Dalton. Lee Boecher, SHORTGRASS COUNTRY [book] (Montana, Pioneer Schools, 1969) p. 16.
12. Death certificate of Cole Dalton. "Obituary of Coleman Dalton," KINGFISHER FREE PRESS, March 2, 1920.
13. Death certificate (delayed filing) Bea Elizabeth Phillips. Death certificate (amended) Jack J. Phillips. Death certificate, Lee Phillips. Birth certificate, Brent Dalton Phillips. George Phillips Bible. Numerous personal conversations and letters with Bill Phillips, Mrs. Annie Phillips and other members of the Phillips family.
14. Death certificate, Littleton Dalton.
15. "More Bloodshed In The Indian Territory. " THE COFFEYVILLE DAILY JOURNAL. December 1, 1887. "A Terrible Tragedy. Two Men and One Woman Are Killed And Two Men Wounded" Newspaper clipping, name of newspaper not shown. December 2, 1887.
16. "The Last Of The Daltons Returns to Coffeyville and Points Out Scenes of Their Last Bank Raid", KANSAS CITY STAR, May 10, 1931.
17. "Gracie May Rhodes", SANTA ROSA REPUBLICAN, May 2, 1948, Sunset View Cemetery Records.
18. Marriage license of Eva Dalton and J. N. Whipple. "Eva May Whipple" KINGFISHER FREE PRESS, January 30, 1839. Maggie Aldridge Smith, SILOAM SPRINGS HISTORY VOL I,[book] (1970) p. 123, 414.
19. "Killed By a Marshal's Posse", THE COFFEYVILLE JOURNAL, August 16, 1888.
20. Death certificates of Emmett Dalton, Julia Dalton Johnson, Jennie May Perrier, Raymond H. Coombs, Genio Kenneth Coombs. Marriage license of Emmett Dalton and Julia Lewis. Eastern Cherokees Application of Jennie May Gilstrap. Baptism Record of Emmett Dalton. "Widow of Famed Robber Dies In Fresno Hospital", THE FRESNO BEE, May 21, 1943. "Last Member of Dalton Gang Dies of Long Illness", LOS ANGELES TIMES, July 14, 1937. "Last Dalton Aids State", LOS ANGELES TIMES, November 1, 1 935. Letter dated July 3, 1937 from Charles M. Martin, Oceanside California to Mr. N. H. Rose, San Antonio, Texas, subject, Emmett Dalton. Personal interview with granddaughter of Julia Dalton, April 1989.
21. Death certificate, Leona Randolph Dalton. "Leona Dalton Dies, Funeral Scheduled Tuesday Morning", KINGFISHER FREE PRESS, April 29, 1964. Lee Boecher, op.cit. 14-18. Personal interview with Shirley Smith (sister of Lee Boecher and personal friend of Leona Dalton), April 1989.

22. "Married-Clute-Dalton", THE KINGFISHER FREE PRESS, January 30, 1896. " Mrs. Nannie Dalton Clute ", THE KINGFISHER FREE PRESS. January 2, 1902. Death certificate of Roy Clute. Lee Boecher, op. cit. p. 14.
23. Army records of Simon Noel Dalton. Marriage license S. M. Dalton and Minnie McDaniel. Bastardy case, Nowata, Co. Ok. February 7, 1910, Minnie Mc Daniel. Federal Census, 1910, Nowata, Co. Ok. shows Minnie's son as Jean F. Mc Daniel. Death certificate, Sam Dalton. Lee Boecher, op. cit. p.13-16.
All dates of births, deaths, and marriages were taken from the applicable record where available. Dates do not always agree and where two or more records give the same date that date is used, otherwise it is a judgment call on the part of the author. Example: The newspaper gives one date for the date of death for Nancy Dalton Clute, the tombstone another. I have used the date on the tombstone because I thought it most likely a family member who had the best available information would have furnished that date.

Bob and Grat Dalton in death after the Coffeyville Raid.

The Dalton Gang in death after the Coffeyville Raid, Bill Powers, Bob Dalton, Grat Dalton and Dick Broadwell.

The following story is reprinted with permission from the *Hutchinson Herald,* September 28, 1952. This was written when the Dalton Gang Hideout was a new attraction and still big news in the Southwest Kansas area.

Although we have since disproved some of the facts, it makes for a great story and we truly believe Mr. Dewey based it on actual happenings as told to him by local citizens.

Gay Little Eva Not Quite So Innocent

By Ernest Dewey

Meade - When Eva Dalton, the town milliner, married J. N. Whipple on Oct. 25, 1887, the occasion was one of considerable regret among the young bachelors of the community. Pretty Eva was a popular partner at sociables, a gay and energetic dancer at local hoedowns.

Whipple was the town's first merchant and a proficient poker player. He had moved his general store to Meade after the town of Tusland drilled 200 feet for water and didn't find any.

The bride's youngest brother, Emmett, attended the wedding dressed in pistols. That attracted no attention, then, for almost everybody wore them.

The couple were visited and congratulated soon after by Eva's brothers, Bob and Grat, deputy marshals for the federal court of "Hanging Judge" Parker, who were working industriously with the famous jurist to stamp out outlawry in the Indian Territory. Certain critics remarked that Bob and Grat served their warrants mostly on desperadoes who were rather dead and the loot always disappeared. These suspicions were disregarded as unworthy.

The newlywed Whipples moved into a new house, a tiny two-roomed frame structure on the side of a hill set above a larger two-roomed basement with an outside entrance on the lower level. This architecture, although somewhat odd, aroused no interest. Lumber was scarce and expensive. Whipple probably was considered smart in saving wood by making the largest portion of his home a dug-out.

Storekeeping appeared to bore Whipple and soon he gave it up to devote more time and attention to his poker-playing. Despite uncertainties and hazards of the game, the Whipples continued prosperous. Eva blossomed with a matched team and a shiny black buggy to match her sparkling eyes. The pair also sported several fine riding horses although suspicious persons noted these weren't always the same horses. The Whipples explained airily that they did a lot of trading.

The Whipple's social activities were cut down a little when it became known that Eva's brothers had tossed away their badges as officers of the law in favor of quicker profits from robbing banks, travelers, and trains. Exploits of the famous Dalton gang were on everybody's lips but Eva's. Most of her neighbors agreed that it was a crying shame her brothers had gone to the bad, but it was not her fault. It was with grim, pressed lips she received the news, on Oct. 4, 1892, that the Dalton gang had been wiped out at Coffeyville in an over-ambitious effort to rob two banks at once. Bob and Grat were dead. Emmett was wounded. Another brother, Bill, was first reported killed. Later it was learned that, for some unaccountable reason, he had not accompanied the gang that day.

Eva received expressions of sympathy in rather non-committal fashion, appeared to want to forget it, so kindly neighbors said. Excitement died down but it flared again on May 28, 1893. That day the Doolin gang, with which Bill Dalton had joined forces, held up and robbed a Santa Fe train at Cimarron and headed south toward sister Eva's home at Meade.

A few miles northeast of Meade the train robbers took dinner, at gun point, with the J. H. Randolph family. They were last seen about two miles east of Meade. There the trail vanished.

The home of the Whipples was watched but there was no sign of visitors or illegal enterprise. Eva went about her housewifely duties and Whipple about his poker playing as usual. If contact was made with the bandit gang or any were harbored in the hillside house, no eye was sharp enough to detect anything. The law made an apologetic examination of the premises, under Eva's unwelcoming eyes. It seemed plain that no one else was inhabiting the premises although the Whipples owned more horses than usual that day.

When the fuss died down the Whipples moved away, abandoning their property. Some said they were driven out of town by unkind suspicion.

Finally, at a tax foreclosure sale, the property was sold. The H. G. Marshall family moved into the house.

Eating a late meal one evening, the Marshalls were startled by the appearance of an unexpected guest right beside their table. The intruder was travel-stained, dusty, and rough-looking. He regarded the Marshalls with obvious surprise, made an uncertain but threatening motion with the Winchester he carried in his hand, then vanished as mysteriously as he had appeared into a hole underneath the stairway.

When sure their visitor was gone, the Marshalls investigated. They found behind a concealed doorway, a long tunnel large enough for a man to walk through by stooping slightly. It led from the house to the barn where another door was concealed by a feed bin. During the family's residence in the house several riders rode into the barn, put up their horses, and came on into the house through the tunnel. On finding strangers occupying the place, these impulsive visitors quickly fled back through the tunnel, remounted their horses, and galloped away. Gay little Eva apparently was not so innocent as she seemed.

The Dalton Gang and Their Family Ties

Eva Dalton Whipple's hideout house for her rascally brothers and their desperado associates still stands in Meade, just as it did in 1887, three blocks south of the town's main street. The now-famous escape tunnel has been restored and thousands of visitors annually follow the footsteps of the Daltons through the passageway to come out in the barn and view the equally famous Walter Dingess gun collection, West Kansas relics of pioneer days, and an extensive display of photographs of legendary figures out of the Kansas past. Among these photographs are included, of course, the Daltons.

An introduction to Belle Mackey....

by Nancy Ohnick

The following story was taken from a newspaper clipping found in an old scrapbook. The clipping was from the *Meade Globe Press* printed sometime in 1941. The reporter had interviewed Mrs. Belle Mackey, who would have been seventy-six years old at the time. This kind of eye-witness account is very important to us because it is all the proof we have to place members of the Dalton Gang in or near Meade where their sister, Eva, lived at the time.

The Mackey Ranch was south of Meade located on a tract of land bisected by the Cimarron in Beaver County, Oklahoma, and Meade County, Kansas. No Man's Land, was the common name given to this area—no one owned it, there was no law and order, making it a favorite place for the lawless.

This story was of particular interest to me as my grandmother, Kathrine Feldman, worked for Mrs. Mackey when she was a very young girl. My father recalls her telling that she went to work on the Mackey ranch at the age of six, herding cattle, and later, during her teen years, she helped with the housework. She would have been twelve years old in 1892, and very well could have been at the ranch when this story took place.

If you are not familiar with this portion of Oklahoma, you might picture in your mind sparsely populated pastureland, flat for the most part with rolling hills. The vegetation is buffalo grass, soap weed, and sage brush, with a few cactus here and there, few, if any, trees would dot the landscape. The Mackey home was a sod house and very small by today's standards.

An old sod house on the plains... the Mackey home would have looked much like this one.

Emmett Dalton Was Her Guest For Two Days

One morning in February, 1892, when the blue haze hung particularly heavy over the Cimarron River and the luscious hay meadow, so heavy that the sound of horses' feet was deadened until you were unaware that horsemen were near, a young man slid off his horse at the Dave Mackey ranch south of Meade so exhausted he could hardly stand. He asked for something to eat. His eyes gave off a wild look as he gazed at Mr. Mackey and his young wife as though he was making up his mind whether to stop or attempt to make his way farther along the river. He had come from south of the Mackey place in Oklahoma.

The young man of near 20 years was boyish looking and had a harassed look. Mr. Mackey took in the situation and asked him to light and come in the house for something to eat. His wariness was not entirely satisfied as he came into the house, but his strength was spent and he dropped on a cot. His body was wracked with fever, but he accepted the kindly ministrations of Mr. and Mrs. Mackey and permitted them to offer some care. He told them he was suffering with LaGrippe, known as influenza and now called flu.

The quick eye of Mr. Mackey took in far more than the young man revealed to Mr. and Mrs. Mackey. They knew they were entertaining an outlaw, but what outlaw they did not know. The bullet-scarred horse, bullet holes through his coat, his heavy revolvers, and long-distance rifle told them far more than words he could have spoken. The practiced eye and keen observation were essential to the pioneers' life and ability to remain atop of bad men who continually roamed this part of the county.

To have asked his name, they would have been met by a rebuff and suspicion. It was not until the following fall after the Coffeyville bank robbery by the Dalton Gang, that Mr. and Mrs. Mackey learned the name of the young man who had been their visitor the year before. When they saw in the newspapers the photos of the bank robbers, they knew their guest for two days had been Emmett Dalton.

When young Dalton insisted he was ready to travel, he made known his wishes and suddenly discovered that his loaded guns were not under the bedclothes where he remembered putting them. He sprang from the cot, but Mrs. Mackey was just as quick and warned him that if he approached another step toward her, she would shoot.

She was tremulous in her knees, but in those days the young mother with two young children was always ready to defend their own. Mrs. Mackey told young Dalton that when he was ready to leave he could have the guns, that he was perfectly safe in their hut. Evidently he was satisfied, for he went back to his cot and the next day rode away after thanking Mr. and Mrs. Mackey for their kind attentions.

Dalton was at the Mackey home for two days and one night. While he was there several cowboys approached the house. He was quite uneasy about them until Mr. and Mrs. Mackey assured him they were men from another nearby ranch, but he was anxious that these men not learn he was in hiding about the place. Dalton told Mr. Mackey that he had robbed a bank and got in pretty close quarters. When he left the Mackey home he asked that they not watch

which way he rode, but Mrs. Mackey says the temptation was too much and she looked out the window. "But after he was out of sight he could have turned any direction," said Mrs. Mackey.

So far as is known, Mrs. Mackey is the only person living in this community who remembers seeing Emmett Dalton. It is quite possible he appeared on the streets of Meade when his sister Eva Dalton Whipple made her home in Meade. But he did not make his presence known to the citizens.

Breakfast for Three Outlaws

Mrs. Belle Mackey came to Kansas in the early eighties overland from Arizona. The family stopped in route at several places for a short time, but finally landed in this part of the country. As a young lady, Belle met and married David Mackey and they made their home on the Cimarron in 1887.

Mrs. Mackey well remembers one morning when three horsemen rode up to the house and demanded that she get breakfast and feed their horses. Such a command to her was foreign and she refused to comply with the demand. They told her that she would do so or else.

"Mad, I was as mad as a hornet disturbed from its nest," said Mrs. Mackey. "I bustled into the house and took a good look at my one year-old son, Dave, and decided I would get their breakfast but as to feeding their horses never."

Mr. Mackey was not at home, but was with some ranchers gathering cattle.

"I got their breakfast, all the time keeping my head and observing the men. Their rifles and big six-shooters were never far from their hands and I decided that I must do as I was ordered for I did not know what they would do. My first thoughts were for my one year-old son." said Mrs. Mackey, "but feed horses I did not. I told them where the feed was and if they wanted them fed, they would have to do it. I noticed they took the saddle bags off the horses and brought them into the house and at least one man never took his eyes off of them."

"When the men had finished their meal and were ready to leave, they handed me a $100 bill. "That incensed me, too," said Mrs. Mackey, "for a man to offer $100 for three breakfasts. If they had offered me $5.00 for the meals I might have taken it, but in those days we did not charge the wayfaring man for a night's lodging or some meals. The pioneer spirit was strong with those who had for those who had not. When Mr. Mackey came home two days later he told about a train robbery at Cimarron or bank robbery at Spearville. I do not remember which."

[EDITOR'S NOTE: Young Dave Mackey was born in July, 1886. He would have been one year old in the summer of 1887. This is inconsistent with the Dalton-Doolin Gang's robberies in Spearville and/or Cimarron, which took place in 1892 and 1893. Fred Dodge writes of a settler's wife recanting just such a story as this in his book, ***Under Cover for Wells Fargo***, but in 1893 while investigating the Bill Dalton - Bill Doolin Gang. When the gang robbed the Ford County Bank in Spearville, in November, 1892, they got away with $1697.30 much of it in $100 bills. One has to wonder if in telling the story in her old age, Belle Mackey confused the age of her son or confused the news her husband brought home on the occasion. Her daughter, Laura Belle Mackey, was born in May of 1889, she would have been one year old in the spring of 1890.]

When the Daltons Rode

By Bill Phillips

Bill Phillips is the grandson of Elizabeth Dalton, sister to the notorious outlaws. At the time of this writing, Bill still lived in the "Territory of Oklahoma" where so many of the family ended up. The following is his story of the Daltons and his family ties.

The Dalton brothers, there were ten of them, will always be remembered for the misdeeds of the four bad ones, Grat, Bob, Emmett, and Bill. They rode across the Cherokee Strip a century ago and provided a never-ending source of stories for the newspapers of the day, while most of the Dalton family led honest and sedentary lives in the Kingfisher area. The three brothers were credited with shootings and robberies from one end of the country to the other.

The rumor that the Daltons might be headed for a particular town struck terror in the hearts of its businessmen. Those who claimed to know said one good reason why the Daltons were the way they were was because of their bad blood.

Adeline Younger Dalton, mother of the clan, was the aunt of another family of outlaws, the Youngers. Her nephews, Cole, Bob, and Jim, rode the outlaw trail in the fashion of some more of their relatives, Frank and Jesse James.

The Dalton boys were the sons of James Lewis and AdelineYounger Dalton, who had brought them out of Missouri at the start of the Civil War and settled the family on a farm near Coffeyville, Kansas, just north of the Indian Territory. It was a wild and lawless frontier town where the young boys grew up on the tales of their outlaw relatives.

When the new Oklahoma Territory was opened in 1889, the Dalton family joined the land rush and the father and older sons obtained claims near Kingfisher, Oklahoma.

The claim that James and Adeline Dalton chose was the SW 1/4 of sec. 11, in township 17, north of Range 8, west of the Indian Meridian in Oklahoma. This claim contained 160 acres, all bottom land, 6 miles northeast of the town of Kingfisher, Oklahoma. Times were hard in the new raw land. James Lewis Dalton, father of the clan, returned to Kansas to work in Coffeyville while Mrs. Dalton remained on the claim with the children to prove it up.

James Lewis Dalton died in 1890, leaving the family on their own. He was buried at the Robbins Cemetery in Dearing, Kansas, near Coffeyville.

Four of the sons served as deputy marshals from time to time while the fifth moved to Montana and eventually to California. Bill Dalton served with the State of California two terms. Charles, Ben and Littleton Dalton took claims near Kingfisher. Henry Coleman Dalton participated in the Cherokee Strip land rush and took a claim near Enid, Oklahoma.

Frank, one of the elder of the brothers, was killed in 1887 while serving as a deputy in a fight with Indian horse thieves in Indian Territory. Another brother, Gratton, usually called Grat, also became a lawman. He was wounded while on duty in 1888. Bob and Emmett served as deputies for a time, but gradually they drifted to the other side of the law.

Bob was the wild one. While still a deputy; he killed a man in a lover's quarrel and secretly organized an outlaw gang of horse thieves.

When some horses which had disappeared in Indian Territory turned up in Kansas, suspicion fell on the Dalton brothers, who decided to take a vacation and visit their brother, Bill, in California. It was not a quiet vacation, however, because on the night of February 6, 1891, the Southern Pacific passenger train was stopped south of Tulare, California, and held up by masked gunmen.

Lawmen trailed Grat to his brother's home and arrested both men. Bill proved his alibi and got off, but Grat was identified as one of the bandits and sentenced to Folsom Prison. He escaped while in route to prison and, with Emmett, fled back to Oklahoma.

Bob organized the gang with his brothers and three cowboys, Bill Doolin, Dick Broadwell, and Bill Powers. They were later joined by Blackface Charley Bryant, a cowboy from near Hennessey. On May 9, they held up the Santa Fe train at Wharton. A posse that chased them after the holdup was ambushed near Twin Mounds and one of its members killed.

The gang messed up again a year later, this time to rob the Santa Fe train at Red Rock. It was a text-book holdup, patterned after those the James gang had perfected years earlier in Missouri. Bryant was arrested near Hennessey and killed in a shoot out with Deputy Ed Short on the train platform in Waukomis.

The gang next hit the Katy at Adair, where they exchanged gunfire with guards on the train. They rode off to a hideout along the Cimarron, not to be heard of again until their attempt to rob two banks at one time in their old hometown of Coffeyville, Kansas.

From the Dalton cave near Mannford they set out one frosty October morning. Six of them trailed north, Bob, Grat, Emmett Dalton, Bill Powers, Dick Broadwell, and Bill Doolin, taking their time, camping in a little draw north of Coffeyville on October 4, 1892.

On the morning of October 5, they headed for town. Doolin's horse pulled up lame and he stopped to steal another. The others went on into town to complete the holdup, with Doolin promising to follow shortly.

Grat Dalton, Bill Powers and Dick Broadwell hit the C. M. Condon Bank, while Bob and Emmett Dalton went into the First National Bank across the street. Alex McKenna, who ran a dry goods and grocery store near by, spotted the men and gave the alarm. Citizens came out of their businesses armed and ready for a fight.

The battle that followed lasted only 12 minutes. In the hail of bullets, along with four Coffeyville citizens. Bill Doolin, on his way to town to join his companions, heard about the shootout and quickly fled back to Indian Territory. Emmett, though gravely wounded, survived and was sent to Kansas State Prison.

Adeline, his mother made one or two trips a year to visit Emmett. During his imprisonment, she also corresponded with the Governor trying to gain his release. Warden Jewett who spoke readily and positively, "I am convinced that Emmett Dalton is not a criminal at heart." Jewett said, "I am just as positive that if he were released tomorrow he would lead a life creditable to the community in which he resided and that the criminal records of Kansas or any other state would never again have his name written upon them."

Emmett was released in 1907, and told reporters, *"I have always refused to talk, not because I did not care to have my version known, but because I feared that if I had given out interviews the public might get the impression that I was fishing for sympathy.*

"Twenty years ago there was a semblance of law but everything was as near wide open as anything could be. Shooting was common; the killing of a man was almost a daily occurrence. "I idolized my brother Bob. 'Bad Man' talk was as common then as law enforcement is today. I was a boy of 16 and was thrown into this atmosphere. Everywhere I went, I drank this talk up. Soon I seemed to become a part of it all and I became a willing listener, although it shocked me at first.

"One day when I was 18, I was with my brother Bob, and he started to make an arrest. The men resisted. Bob told me to 'git' and I was just that young not to have the sense to run. I drew my six-shooter and we arrested and put the men in jail. My not running impressed Bob, and he said afterwards that he wanted me with him in Coffeyville.

"When Bob entered the vault and put $23,000 in a sack and we left out the back door, not a shot was fired. When we reached our horses it seemed everybody in town had opened fire. A bullet hit me in the right shoulder, my right arm was out of commission, my Winchester dropped from my right hand. I didn't kill a soul that day. I couldn't if I had wanted to. My right arm was useless.

" Knowing the others were in trouble, Bob went to help, I looked back to see Bob on the ground with his back to a large rock and went back to help him. I leaned over and got hold of his wrist with my left hand. He was still alive. Just then a load of buckshot struck me in the back. That's the last I remember for I rolled off my horse and hit the ground. I was in bed for 72 days.

" I was advised to plead guilty to murder in the second degree. Judge Jerry McCune sentenced me to life in the penitentiary. If I had run that day when Bob ask me to 'git', chances are I wouldn't have been in the Coffeyville Two Bank attempt gang raid on October 5, 1892."

Emmett was granted a full pardon on November 4, 1907, from Governor Hoch. He was satisfied that Emmett would make good. A government without mercy is weak said the governor. Emmett came to Kingfisher but didn't stay long. He married his childhood sweetheart on September 2, 1908. She was the daughter of "Texan" Johnson. Julia Johnson was among those who worked for his pardon. However, none was more diligent and more earnest that Julia. She talked with those who opposed the pardon and persuaded them to give Emmett another chance.

Emmett went to California and became successful in a building and real estate business. He died on July 13, 1937, in Los Angeles, California, and was cremated and his ashes are buried in the Kingfisher Cemetery in the family plot.

Bill Dalton, the 8th child and the 7th son, was born in Belton, Missouri, in 1863. He married Jane Bliven of Livingston, California. They had two children, Charles Coleman and Gracie. Bill left his family and came to Oklahoma Territory and organized a gang with Bill Doolin.

Bill was staying at a place called Elk, later known as Poolsville, Oklahoma. His wife Jane and children, Charles Coleman and

Gracie, had come down on the train and were all living near Poolsville. On May 23, 1894, the gang robbed the First National Bank of Longview, Texas.

On June 8, 1894, a posse gathered and had ridden all night from Ardmore to reach the secluded house. There were his Charles, 9, and little Gracie, 7, and four other children out in front playing. Bill Dalton walked out on the porch of the old farm house to watch the children play. He stood there for just a minute before spotting the approaching S.T. Lindsey, a U.S. Deputy Marshal, who had gathered up the posse the night before.

Quick as a flash, Bill, on the porch, turned and dived back inside. He grabbed a revolver, ran toward the back of the house, and jumped through a window. Gun in hand, he was running toward a nearby grove of trees when Deputy Loss Hart yelled for him to surrender. He didn't, of course. The fleeing man fell heavily to the ground, falling on his stomach. By the time the officers reached him he had rolled over onto his back. He was asked his name, but the officers said later he only smiled up at them, closed his eyes, and died.

A quick check revealed that the man was carrying $285.00. The posse headed back to the farm house where the six children were huddled together crying. They asked the youngster's names and were surprised when two of them answered with a name they knew all too well *"Dalton"*.

The man they killed that June 8, 1894, day, outside of Ardmore, Oklahoma Territory, was William Marion (Bill) Dalton. Brother of the infamous Dalton gang members and, at the time, probably the country's best-known outlaw. Inside the little house they found $1,700 in bank notes and coin and a bank sack that bore the name of the First National Bank of Longview, Texas.

Yes, it had been Bill Dalton himself who had led the May 23, 1894, bank robbery in Longview that left two townspeople and two bandits dead. News of Dalton's demise spread quickly. Bill Dalton is dead. He died with his boots on and pistols in hand. Died like a hunted tiger, died the death of an outlaw, but died in true glory. Reporters said no doubt the boldest outlaw that ever figured in the western country had passed from the stage of action.

Thomas Lewis Phillips, brother- in-law of the bandits, the grand-father of this author, was joined by several thousand other Oklahomans who pushed their way into Appollas Undertaking establishment to view the outlaw's remains. On June 13, 1894, Jennie Dalton the bandit's 27 year-old widow, took little Charles and Gracie by the hand and boarded a westbound train at midnight. The train pulled away carrying her husband and the children's father toward a final resting place in Livingston, California.

At the time of Dalton's death, rewards for his capture dead or alive totaled $25,000, but the terror of the southwest, the outlaw Bill Dalton, in the yellow suspenders, was to be feared no more. With Bill Dalton out of the way, Oklahoma and the Indian Territory were fully qualified for admission as a state.

Thomas Louis Phillips, my grandfather, and his oldest son, John Phillips, told the story and connection with the outlaw Daltons, about how the outlaw gang visited their sister Elizabeth many times in the Indian Territory days of Oklahoma. When things got tough in the new, raw, lawless, wild Oklahoma Territory land, the Dalton brothers and gang members sometimes would be on the hideout from the law. One of the hideouts was a cave in the tabletop mountains near Foster, Oklahoma.

A proud-to-be-descendant of the Dalton gang, BILL PHILLIPS.

Bill Dalton, Bill Doolin and the Wild Bunch

By Nancy Ohnick and Roger Meyers

After Bob, Grat and Emmett Dalton met their demise in Coffeyville on October 5, 1892, William "Bill" Dalton took up where they left off. Incensed by the treatment his fallen brothers received in Coffeyville, Bill was very vocal as he stayed by brother Emmett's side throughout his recovery and trial. Bill surely seemed to have a chip on his shoulder and it wasn't long before his name started appearing in the newspapers as he embarked on his own outlaw career. He rode with Bill Doolin and several others from his brother's old gang, but the name "Dalton" still held the reputation, giving him credit as leader of the gang, mention of which put fear in the hearts of citizens all over Kansas and Oklahoma.

William (Bill) Doolin was born in 1858, in Johnson County, Arkansas. In 1881, at the age of 23, he drifted west, working odd jobs and eventually ended up in Caldwell, KS, were he met Oscar D. Halsall of Texas.

Halsall hired Doolin to work for him on his ranch on the Cimarron River in Oklahoma, where he soon became a top hand. It was during his time of working as a cowboy that he met most of the members of his future "Wild Bunch" gang, George "Bitter Creek" Newcomb, Charlie Pierce, Bill Power, Dick Broadwell, Bill "Tulsa Jack" Blake, and Emmett Dalton.

Bill Doolin

Doolin's first brush with the law came in the summer of 1891, while working on the Bar X Bar Ranch. Several cowboys decided to celebrate the 4th of July holiday by riding over to Coffeyville, KS, and throwing a party. The party included a keg of beer and prohibition was the law in Kansas at that time. When lawmen tried to confiscate the beer a shoot-out ensued, and two officers were wounded. From that day on Bill Doolin was on the owl hoot trail. He fled the scene and returned to the Cherokee Strip.

By September of 1891, Doolin was riding with the Dalton Gang. He participated in the train robberies at Leliaetta, Indian Territory (IT,) Red Rock, Oklahoma Territory (OT), and Adair, I T. Several reasons have been given as to why Bill Doolin did not join the Dalton Gang on their fatal raid on two banks in Coffeyville, KS, on October 5, 1892. Emmett Dalton later wrote about the break-up, "Doolin, Pierce, and Newcomb were lopped off in such a way as not to create any ill feeling. They simply didn't fit in with our next project, the climax of our career. So that the split-up might have no sting we made a vague future rendezvous with the discarded trio. They rode off together with friendly farewell..." Some say that Bob Dalton considered Doolin too much of a "wildcat" and too uncontrollable, but it turned out to be his good fortune to have split with the Daltons that day.

With the death of the Daltons in Coffeyville, the Wild Bunch didn't waste any time filling their boots. On October 12, 1892, seven days after the raid, eighteen miles west of Coffeyville, the train at Caney, KS, was robbed by four masked men. While never proven, Bill Doolin is credited with the event.

Now on their own, Doolin, Newcomb, and Pierce were looking for new recruits for their gang. The first to join was Oliver "Ol" Yantis. On November 1, 1892, he joined Doolin and Newcomb to rob the Ford County Bank at Spearville, KS. After the robbery the trio split up to throw off any pursuing posse. However, marshals were able to track Yantis to his sister's farm near Orlando, OT, and on November 30, they surprised him at daybreak and killed him in a brief gun battle.

By the end of 1892, four more members had joined the gang, Bill Blake alias "Tulsa Jack," Dan Clifton alias "Dynamite Dick," George "Red Buck" Waightman, and William "Bill" Dalton. By the spring of 1893, the gang was riding high. Their reputation was growing and their activities were becoming ever more bold.

March 14, 1893, Bill Doolin and Edith Ellsworth of Ingalls, OT, were married in Kingfisher, OT. Edith was a preacher's daughter, whether she knew Bill was an outlaw at the time is not known, but throughout his career as an outlaw she stuck by him, all the time keeping the marriage and their time together a secret.

The Dalton-Doolin Gang perpetrated a train robbery at Cimarron, KS, on June 10, 1893. This was the closest to Meade any of the Daltons were known to have committed a crime.

Bill Dalton would have known this area well as his sister, Eva Whipple, lived in Meade from the mid 1880's until early in 1892. The Whipple home was conveniently located on the south edge of Meade along a draw that made it possible for riders from the south to come and go undetected by the town folk or the law. It was suspected but never proven that they offered an occasional hideout for the Dalton brothers during their criminal career. The Whipples had moved back to Oklahoma by the time the Cimarron robbery took place, but it stands to reason if the brothers and other gang members had used the Whipple home for a hideout, they would have known this area well.

Fred Tracy recalled how the gang held up in Beaver, OT, for three days before they headed for Cimarron. "These men obtained meals at the hotel, but slept in the livery stable. They were here for three days. Their horses were kept saddled day and night. During the day three men always remained with their horses. The others never separated and spent the daytime around the saloons. About everyone in Beaver knew who they were and when they met up with them in the saloons, they treated them as they would treat any local resident. No one asked them their names, where they came from or where they were going." The gang left Beaver going north, and it would have been a natural course to travel through Meade, a distance of about forty miles, in a direct line north to Cimarron.

Solomon Zortman had a claim northwest of Fowler, Kansas. Sol told his family down through the years of this gang stopping by their place sometime before the robbery at Cimarron. They stopped around noon and asked to water and feed their horses and Nancy

Zortman asked them to eat with them, which they did. Later, on their way back through, Sol and also a neighbor saw the gang moving fast, they didn't stop this time, nor did they greet the settlers. When they learned of the robbery at Cimarron, the neighbor said, "I had my big 50, if I'da known what they'd done they wouldn't have made it out of Kansas!"

The gang arrived at the Wilson farmstead sixteen miles south of Cimarron on Thursday, June 8, 1893, representing themselves as Texas Rangers hunting horse thieves. There they spent the night. The gang ate dinner and supper Friday with farmer J. H. Lilly near Cimarron. They curried and fed their horses well, and left the farm about dusk. On their way into town, the "Rangers" appropriated a team of horses from the farm of N. A. Leonard. Bill Doolin was a planner; these extra horses would come in handy during the pursuit that would surely follow the robbery. On Friday night, June 9, 1893, Bill Doolin, Bill Dalton, Bitter Creek Newcomb and Tulsa Jack Blake came into Cimarron and prepared for the nights business.

Train No. 3, the "California Express," due at 12:10 AM on Saturday, June 10, pulled into Cimarron a few minutes late. Conductor Bender got off the train and headed inside the depot to check on their orders. Engineer Robinson, the fireman, and the express messenger stayed aboard. Suddenly two men climbed onto the engine, covered Robinson and the fireman with their Winchesters, and ordered them to get the train moving. Simultaneously, two other men boarded the last car of the train. Seeing the train pulling out, conductor Bender rushed out of the depot and managed to jump on the rear of the train where he too was taken hostage.

The train was ordered stopped about one-half mile west of Cimarron. Engineer Robinson and the fireman were told to bring the coal pick from the locomotive and come along to the express car where E.C. Whittlesey guarded the valuables.

When the gang reached the express car, Whittlesey was ordered to open the door. He refused and the fireman was set to work battering it open with the coal pick. All the while the gang sent Winchester bullets into the express car and near the passengers in the other cars. Doolin had learned the art of intimidation. One of the shots fired into the express car seriously wounded express messenger Whittlesey.

After several minutes, the fireman had not made much headway on the door and was told, "Come on, you're a slow son-of-a-bitch; we'll try the engineer." Engineer Robinson was put to the task and soon had the door open. The robbers, using Robinson as a shield, then entered the car and began the search for the loot they knew to be in there. However, the wounded Whittlesey had been busy hiding about $10,000 in cash and jewelry. The gang had to satisfy themselves with the contents of the safe, about $1000 in silver and a small cache of jewelry. "The whole time they were very jovial, joking with the trainmen, telling the engineer they would meet him at the World's fair and treat him," commented the Ingalls Union. Altogether, the robbery took about 40 minutes.

After gathering up the booty, the gang laid Mr. Whittlesey on a cot and gave him a drink of water. Asking if they could do anything else to make him more comfortable, the gang apologized for wounding him. This done, Doolin and the boys mounted up and headed out after telling engineer Robinson not to move the train until he heard a signal shot. Upon hearing the signal shot, the train was backed into the Cimarron station. A Dr. Butcher was called to attend Whittlesey who was taken on to Dodge City, eighteen miles east. Whittlesey recovered and was known to still be working for Wells-Fargo in Trinidad, Colorado, in December of 1914.

The Doolin Gang headed south-southeast, stopping after a short distance to divide the spoils. Gray County Sheriff "Doc" Barton and posse, along with Ford County Sheriff Chalk Beeson set out after daybreak. By this time however, the gang was nearing Meade thirty-six miles south of Cimarron. Already the Santa Fe Rail Road Co. had offered a reward of $1000 for the arrest and conviction of each of the robbers. This reward was raised to $10,000 within a day when Wells Fargo Express Company offered $4000 and the State of Kansas weighed in with $2000.

The gang was in familiar territory around Meade. A few miles northeast of town, the gang stopped at the J. H. Randolph home. There they forced the Randolphs, at gunpoint, to give them dinner. They were last seen about two miles east of Meade heading south.

After the Meade sighting, the gang continued south-southeast and on to Oklahoma on the Healy Trail. As they passed by the Anshutz ranch just south of the Kansas/Oklahoma border, Carrie Anshutz said she noticed the men because they had a loose horse trailing behind them, cowboys always drove their extra horses in front of them. When her husband and young brother rode in a short time later, she asked, "Did you see the outfit that rode by here awhile ago? Who were they?" "That is what we would like to know," Doc Anshutz replied, "but we did not think it healthy to find out for when we started to ride toward them they went through the gate across the river then motioned us to go around and waited with gun in hand until we did so." It wasn't long before news of the train robbery reached the Anshutz place and they knew they had seen the Wild Bunch.

The gang stopped at the Taintor Ranch a short distance south of the Anshutz place for dinner that day, one of the men stayed at the barn with the horses while the others ate. About two hours before the men showed up at the Taintor ranch, a deputy sheriff had been there looking for them. "Better stay awhile," Mr. Taintor remarked jokingly, "they may come in." But the deputy said he had better be getting on. So when they really did come, an hour or two later, the ranch outfit was well aware of who their guests were, but it was obvious these men were desperate and they were heavily armed, so they were given food and allowed to go on.

After they left the Taintor Ranch headquarters they were intercepted by a posse led by Sheriff Frank Healy. Healy and his posse men chased the gang for three miles before the officer's horses became jaded and they abandoned the chase. Indian scouts from Fort Supply, Oklahoma, perhaps accompanying a party of soldiers, then took up the chase. A running battle of several miles resulted in one of the bandit's horses being killed and Bill Doolin wounded in the left foot. Apparently none of the scouts were injured in the battle. Bill Doolin recovered from his wound, but it left him with a limp that plagued him the rest of his life, and it was the contributing factor in his capture years later.

Bill Doolin and his band of raiders returned to Ingalls, Oklahoma Territory, in August where they were joined by "Dynamite Dick"

Clifton, "Arkansas Tom" Jones, and "Red Buck" Weightman. It is said that Doolin sought medical help for his foot from Dr. Duncan Selph in Ingalls. Doolin paid forty dollars for the good doctors treatment and his silence in the matter.

On September 1, 1893, a posse of thirteen men under the command of Deputy U. S. Marshal John Hixon, infiltrated Ingalls in the hope of capturing the Doolin Gang. Doolin, Clifton, Dalton, Blake, and Weightman were in Ransom's Saloon in Ingalls. Bitter Creek Newcomb was mounted on his horse outside when he was alerted to the presence of lawmen in town. Posseman Dick Speed, after having Newcomb pointed out to him, shot Bitter Creek in the leg. The wounded Newcomb fired back, laid spurs to his horse, and headed south out of town. A wild firefight immediately began between the gang in the saloon and the officers. Arkansas Tom heard the shots from his second floor room in the O.K. Hotel where he had gone with an illness. He jumped up and began a deadly accurate sniping. Doolin and the boys in the saloon knew that they had to make a break for it and Daugherty's firing provided the cover they needed. The five men bolted from the rear of the liquor hall to the livery stable several yards behind, spraying bullets at the lawmen as they ran. Upon reaching the stable, Doolin and Clifton saddled the horses while Dalton, Blake, and Weightman kept the lawmen at bay.

Mounting up, the five outlaws burst through the open door of Ransom's Livery and headed southwest. However, a barb-wire fence blocked the way. Marshal Hixon drilled Dalton's horse in the jaw with a Winchester round and another bullet from posseman Lafe Shadley's rifle broke the horse's leg, taking it down. Dalton snatched up the saddlebags containing wire cutters and went to work on a barbed-wire fence. Getting it cut, the five men galloped off to the southeast, Clifton taking a bullet in the neck in the process. Arkansas Tom now needed to be dealt with.

Posseman Jim Masterson came up with two sticks of dynamite and threatened to blow up the hotel if Arkansas Tom did not surrender. Realizing he had been abandoned by the rest of the gang, he agreed to come out. Arkansas Tom was the only prisoner the marshals had to show for the hell they had been through. Posse members Lafe Shadley, Tom Speed, and Tom Hueston were killed in the gunfight along with citizen Del Simmons, and a man named N.A. Walker.

Arkansas Tom was subsequently sentenced to 50 years in the Kansas State Prison in Lansing, being paroled in 1910. Daugherty was eventually killed by Joplin, Missouri law officers in 1924. Although no one was ever tried for the Cimarron Train Robbery, those involved were dead within three years.

In early 1894, the gang was hard at work. Two more members, William F. Raidler (a.k.a. Little Bill) and Richard West (a.k.a. Little Dick) had joined the Wild Bunch. They robbed the Farmers and Citizens Bank in Pawnee, OT, on January 23, 1894. On March 13,1894, two men robbed the railroad station at Woodward, OT, it was believed to be Bill Doolin and Bill Dalton.

May 10, 1894, seven members of the Wild Bunch robbed the bank in Southwest City, Missouri. In the shoot-out with townsfolk one of the bandits was wounded, one citizen was killed, and three were wounded. Bill Dalton was not present at the Southwest City robbery, he had left the Wild Bunch and formed his own gang that spring.

On May 23, 1894 Jim Wallace, Big Asa Knight, Jim Knight, and George Bennett joined up with Bill Dalton to rob the First National Bank in Longview, TX. Bennett and one citizen were killed and three were wounded in the attempted getaway. The law trailed Bill Dalton to his hideout near Ardmore, I T, surprised and killed him on the morning of June 8, 1894. Surprised by Deputy Marshal Loss Hart, Dalton dove through the back window of his house and began running. He was ordered to halt; his answer was to turn and raise his six-shooter. Hart mortally wounded Dalton with a Winchester bullet.

On April 3, 1895, the Wild Bunch pulled off their last job as a gang. They boarded the train at Dover, OT, and proceeded to rob the train and the passengers. After the robbery the gang made their way west at a leisurely pace unaware that a posse had formed and was fast moving in on them. At 2:00 p.m. the posse caught up with the gang as they were camped near Ames, OT. In the gun battle with the deputies Tulsa Jack was killed. The rest of the gang was able to get away, but they split up and never reunited as a gang.

With high rewards on their heads, the gang scattered. The marshals were now using a new tactic in their effort to rid the territory of these lawless men. They used the reward money and outstanding warrants for cattle rustling to induce the Dunns to give them information as to the movements of the gang. The Dunns had a farm near Ingalls, and were never part of the gang. However, they did give the gang a place to hide and information about the deputies, as well as fence some of their stolen goods.

On May 1, 1895, while hiding out at the Dunn farm, Bitter Creek Newcomb and Charlie Pierce were shot while they lay asleep in their beds, by Bill, John, and Dal Dunn. They took the bodies to Guthrie and turned them over to the marshal for $5,000 reward money.

With his buddies dying off one by one, Bill Doolin could see his days were numbered. He had his lawyers get in touch with US Deputy Marshall Nix three times that summer and offered to turn himself in if Marshal Nix would promise him a light sentence on robbery. Marshal Nix refused. The only thing left for Doolin was to leave the territory.

He made his way to New Mexico and joined up with Little Dick West. Together they hid out there the rest of the summer of 1895. On September 6,1895, the law was able to bring another member of the gang to justice. Bill Raidler was seriously wounded and captured by Marshal Bill Tilghman near Pawhuska, OT. He stood trial for his part in the Dover robbery and was found guilty, sentenced to ten years. Raidler was paroled in 1903, and returned to Oklahoma.

Tiring of New Mexico, Doolin returned to Oklahoma to gather his family. By this time Bill and Edith had a son. Together with his family he set out to make a new life for himself. They lived the last part of 1895, near Burden, KS. But the law wasn't finished with Bill Doolin. Deputy Marshal Tilghman learned of Edith Doolin's disappearance from the Ingalls area, and was able to trail her to Burden. However, he was to late, Edith had returned to Oklahoma and a man named "Tom Wilson" had gone to Eureka Springs, Arkansas, to seek the healing treatment of the hot spas there to ease the pain of his rheumatism.

Tilghman suspected it was Doolin and proceeded to Eureka Springs were he did indeed find Doolin and was able to capture him. He returned him to Guthrie and for the first time in his life Bill Doolin was behind bars. With Bill Doolin behind bars the rest of the gang was rounded up quickly. Red Buck Waightman was killed in gun battle with deputy marshals near Arapaho, OT, on March 4, 1896. Dynamite Dick Clifton was arrested on a whiskey charge in Texas. Deputy Marshal Frank Canton brought him back to Oklahoma to face a murder charge, delivering him to the Guthrie jail on June 22, 1896. Thanks to the law Bill Doolin and Dynamite Dick were back together.

On July 5, 1896, Bill Doolin, Dynamite Dick, and twelve other prisoners escaped from the Guthrie jail. Outside the jail Doolin was able to make it back to Lawson, OT, were Edith was staying with her folks. Once again they made plans to leave the territory and make a new start for their family somewhere else. Once again the law was chasing him. Deputy U. S. Marshal Heck Thomas learned of his whereabouts and with a posse set up an ambush near Doolin's in-laws' home. On August 25, Doolin came walking down the road west from the house. Thomas shouted "Halt, Bill!" Instead of surrendering, Doolin snapped off a shot from his Winchester in the direction of the voice. Before he could fire again, one of the posse killed him with a blast from an eight-gauge shotgun.

Dynamite Dick Clifton and Little Dick West were all that was left of the Wild Bunch. They joined up with the Jennings Gang but later left that gang and eventually were tracked down and killed by the law. Dynamite Dick Clifton was killed by deputies on November 7, 1897, near Chectoah. Little Dick West was killed on April 8, 1898 by Deputy Marshal Heck Thomas's posse.

Bill Dalton in death.

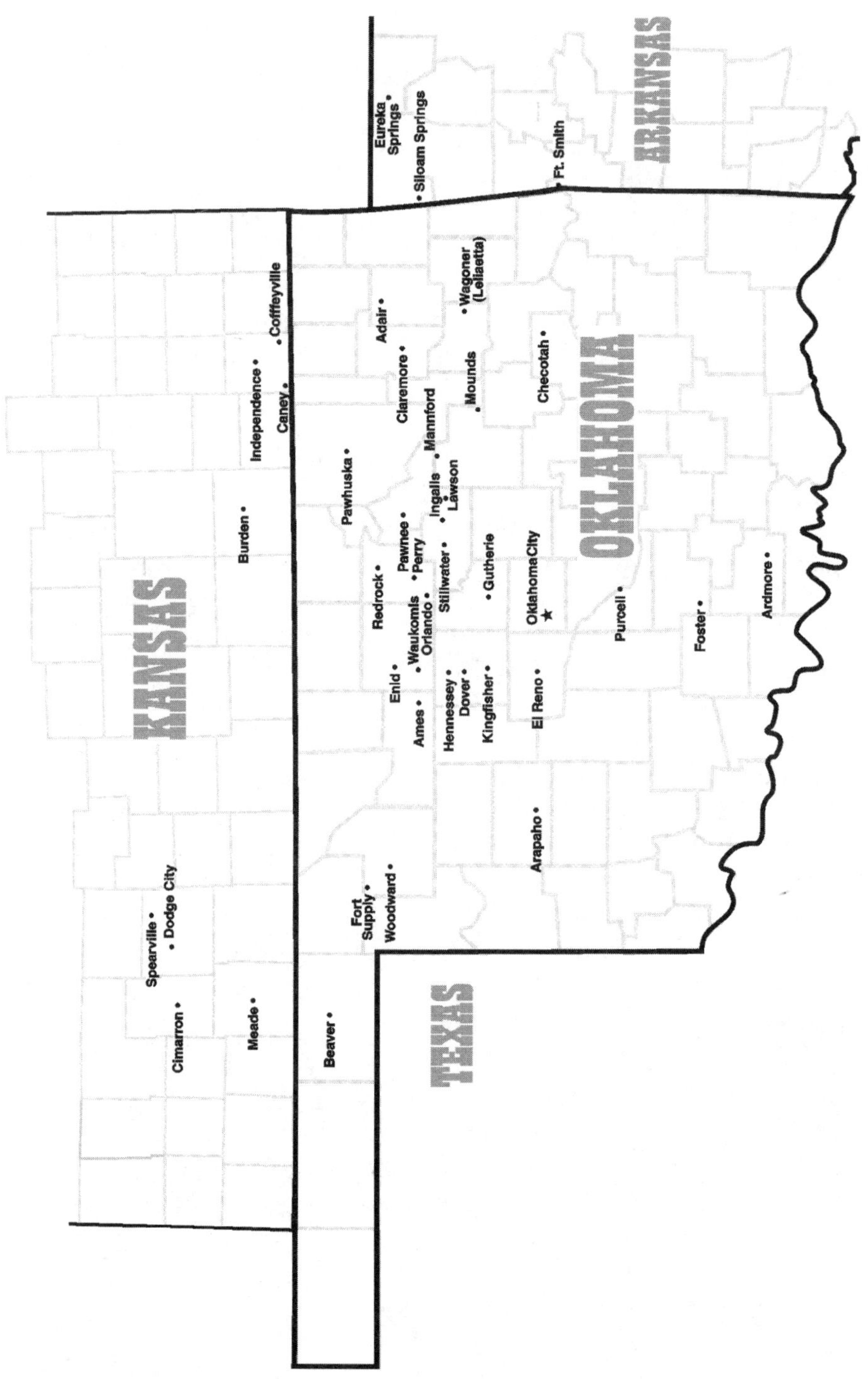
ARKANSAS
Eureka Springs
Siloam Springs
Ft. Smith
Wagoner (Leliaetta)
Adair
Claremore
Mounds
Checotah
Cofffeyville
Independence
Caney
Pawhuska
Mannford
Ingalls
Lawson
Burden
Pawnee
Perry
Stillwater
Redrock
Waukomis
Orlando
Gutherie
Oklahoma City
OKLAHOMA
KANSAS
Purcell
Foster
Ardmore
Enid
Ames
Hennessey
Dover
Kingfisher
El Reno
Arapaho
Fort Supply
Woodward
Spearville
Dodge City
Cimarron
Meade
Beaver
TEXAS

Reprinted with permission, a Newspaper account of Bill Daltons demise from the ***Daily Ardmoreite,*** Saturday, June 9, 1894:

BILL DALTON DEAD
THE NOTED BANK AND TRAIN
ROBBER BROUGHT DOWN
BY A WINCHESTER BALL
NEAR ELK YESTERDAY MORNING
HIS IDENTITY POSITIVELY ESTABLISHED
HIS BODY HERE
THE WIFE OF THE DEAD BANDIT,
DEEPLY AFFECTED, TELLS THE STORY

The Rewards, Aggregating $25,000 Will be paid to the Brave officers The country Can Now draw a Sigh of Relief for the Terror of the West is no More

The rest of the Gang will be caught.

Bill Dalton is dead, he died with his boots on and pistol in hand; died like a hunted tiger, died the death of an outlaw but died true glory. This has been flashed from Ardmore to every point in the United States compassed by wire and no doubt the boldest outlaw that ever figured in the western country has passed from the stage of action, which has cost the express companies millions and banks from Kansas City to Galveston on the south and San Francisco on the west to breath easier knowing this man of terror is not more. For some weeks it has been almost positively known that a band of thieves were making the country between Healdon and Elk headquarters and that section has been closely watched since the Longview bank robbery. This suspicion was deduced to a certainty Thursday when Houston Wallace, well known here, and two strange women came to town and began to spend money very freely. Wallace was known to be a man of limited means and doubtful integrity, so when he was seen to possess money in profusion, his every step was watched. The women gave their names as Mrs. Brown and Miss Pruit. After spending $200 or more at various and sundry places, Wallace went to the express office and obtained a box of suspicious appearance, which gave an excuse for arrest. He was taken into custody and the box found to contain three gallons of whiskey. He was held on a charge of introducing and placed in jail, the women were also held under guard.

Their purchases consisted of an unusual amount of Winchester cartridges of assorted calibers, dress goods, jewelry, groceries suited to camp life and a complete camping outfit.

Deputy Freeman noticed the box of whiskey and told Deputy Lindsey and the two made the arrest. After the first arrest, the women maintained a stolid silence, as did Wallace.

Acting on a suspicion and a strong clue Deputy Lindsey as captain organized a posse consisting of the following well known fearless officers: C.L. Hart, J.H. Lothomen, C.R. Denton, J.H. Reynolds, D.E. Booker, W. B. Freeman, W.H. Clover and R. W. Roberts. They left that evening and rode all night arriving at the house of Houston Wallace Friday morning at 8 o'clock, where the posse divided into squads to reconnoiter the premises. Everything around the house seemed quiet, no unusual stirring about being noticeable. All seen were some women, and children playing in the yard. A slow and prearranged advance was made on the house and when within 200 yards of the place, a woman was driving in some calves and came upon the squads. She tried to maintain her composure and went to the house, thinking that was unguarded. In this she was mistaken for there stood Loss Hart, true game and dead shot. Hart called to Dalton to surrender but instead of throwing up his hands he ducked his head and started for the timber where no doubt then Loss called "surrender." Dalton went for his gun, but he was too late for Hart fired, his ball going true to the mark, entered the vitals, and Dalton fell prostrate and dying. He made but one movement and that was to turn from his face to his back, when the officers got to him he was dead. Deputy Lindsay spied another man at a window in the house and threw down on him. He had pistol in hand but disappeared and it is not known what became of him. The women were told to leave the house, which they lost no time in doing, repairing to the barn. The officers then advanced on the house, and on entering failed to find any other occupants. What became of the other man remains a mystery. Once in the house a search was begun. Everything was in confusion. Money was found in every conceivable place and strange to say without attempt at hiding. The amount of money recovered was not definitely known. Dalton had $285 on his person, and it is stated semi-authentically that about $1700 was recovered. One thing is a settled fact, a money sack with the brand of the Longview bank was captured settling beyond any question of doubt that Dalton was one of the band. The identity of the dead man was fully established by a package of letters found in Mrs. Dalton alias Brown's trunk, from the now dead robber to his wife and addressed to her at Fresno and New Alamode, California. There were also found in the room all kinds of firearms except Winchesters. Strange as it may seem Dalton was undoubtedly caught napping, as he only had his six-shooter and was given no opportunity to use that. This man the terror of the west was laid low with a single shot fired.

The rewards outstanding for capture of Dalton it is thought would aggregate $25,000, which will go to the brave officers who took their lives in their hands to effect his capture.

The remains were taken in charge, placed in a wagon, and the march homeward commenced. About five miles from town Mrs. Dalton and Miss Pruitt who had been released were met and told that Bill Dalton had been killed. Mrs. Dalton at first disclaimed any knowledge of Dalton or what was meant, but in a few moments she broke completely down and in a fit of weeping, said she was Mrs. Dalton, and in piteous cries bemoaned the death of her husband. Her grief was most affecting when the wagon bearing the corpse came up, she was placed in the buggy and returned to the city, going directly to Undertaker Appollas' establishment, where she ordered his body embalmed and prepared in the very best style for shipment. A curious crowd surrounded the place to get a glimpse of her. The Ardmoreite reporter approached her but her lips were sealed against an interview. The only thing she would say was, "all I want is to be left alone in my grief." In a few moments the corpse was driven up and fully 1,000 people pushed and jammed in and around the building so that it was almost impossible to get inside with the remains. This reporter was there, and for the first time in life, beheld what was left of a real train and bank robber. The dead man was placed on a stretcher. He was undoubtedly a fine specimen of physical manhood, being about five feet-eight, and weighing about 165 to 175 pounds, and is twenty-nine years of age.

The widowed wife of a few hours was taken to the Sherman Hotel and given comfortable apartments. Here another attempt at an interview failed. She wired her mother in California and it is understood will ship the remains there for interment. She is a women above the ordinary intelligence and perfectly lady-like in her deportment. She says Bill Dalton was her husband and that she loved him. She is the mother of two children, which are now at Houston Wallace's place. On her return here she immediately sent for her attorneys, Mr. Dick and Brown and placed the management of her affairs in their hands. They are using every endeavor to see that she is not imposed upon nor unnecessarily harassed by the idle curiosity of spectators. That her interest will be ably guarded by them, goes without saying. They have been very diligent in receiving and carrying out her instructions just as earnestly as though she had been the wife of the most prominent man of the nation in similar condition. It is learned she was open in her confession of identity of the dead man and gave them a detailed history of the varied scenes of her eventful life.

A traveling fakir, who was in the city yesterday when the news of Dalton's capture was first brought in, said that if it was Bill Dalton he could identify him. He then described him in detail and when the body was examined his description and the man corresponded exactly. He viewed the remains and made affidavit to the above affect.

MRS. DALTON TALKS

Though unable to have a personal interview with Mrs. Dalton, the Admoreite has, from a reliable source, the following bit of her's and Bill's family history. My maiden name was Jennie Bleven, and twenty-seven years ago was born in Lake County, California, met Bill Dalton in California and married him in 1884, in Merced County, that state. At that time he was wealthy. He served two terms in the California legislature from Merced County. We lived there after marriage about six years. I have two children, a boy nine and a girl seven years old. Their names are Charles and Gracie. My husband has five living brothers. They are Charles, aged forty-three; Coleman, forty; Littleton, thirty-eight; Simon, fifteen and Emmett, who is serving a life sentence in Lansing Penitentiary. Of these Charlie lives in Kingfisher County, Oklahoma, and the younger one with his mother in the same county. There are four sisters of whom two are at home with their mother, aged twenty and eighteen years respectfully. The others, Mrs. Whipple, lives near Kingfisher, age twenty seven, and Mrs. Elizabeth Phillips who lives north of Ardmore in the community of Tussey, her age is thirty-eight. She will not talk of the history of Bill since he began to lead a life of crime, nor drop a word that will throw light on the identity of his comrades. One of them is known possible to be Jim Wallace, brother of Houston Wallace now in jail.

Mrs. Dalton wired her brother in California, also his mother and brother in Kingfisher. Some of them are expected to arrive here tonight. The bank officers at Longview have also been notified and will be here tonight.

THE BODY VIEWED

All day hundreds of people have crowded around Appollas' undertaking establishment where the body lies in state, embalmed subject to the orders of the sorrowing widow. The people came from the country in gangs and throughout the day knots of men could be seen together earnestly discussing the one topic of conversation. It was Dalton in a thousand different forms. There are, as natural consequence, doubting Thomases who know it was not Dalton and there were others who would knowingly nod their heads, blink their eyes and say, "I know lots," but that was all they would tell.

Of one thing there can be no doubt, one of the Longview bank robbers is dead and there is little, in fact we think none at all, but he is Bill Dalton for whose head large rewards are standing today and to which the brave officers are entitled. They have earned it and at the same time sustained their reputation for bravery and fearless vigilance in the discharge of their duty. Captain Lindsay speaks in the highest terms of praise of each one of his posse and says he has every reason to feel proud of their distinguished honors. Los Hart is commended on every hand for the manner in which he has added laurels to his reputation for bravery and at the same time added largely to his exchequer when rewards are paid.

Along The Road

by Nancy Ohnick

A special thanks to Tom Flowers and Mark Goldsberry for their assistance with this article. Tom works for the Soil Conservation District and Mark works for the Kansas Wildlife and Parks Department.

When I travel I am constantly intrigued by the wild flowers, trees and natural wonders I see out my car window. For those of you not familiar with Southwest Kansas, I will attempt to describe to you what you will see while driving through Meade County.

You enter Meade County about five miles east of Fowler, and about two miles west of Plains when traveling US Highway 54. You will find our county diverse in landscape with pasture and crop land alternating continuously from the sandy, dry land in the east to lush, irrigated fields in the west.

If you are traveling in the spring...

Wheat is our main crop and in early spring will appear green and look much like fields of grass. You may see cattle grazing on winter wheat pastures up until early May when the wheat starts to "head out" or develop the grains. The wheat heads grow at the end of long stems and can look like a sea waving in the wind.

We start to plant corn, milo and soybeans in late spring. Alfalfa fields will be dark green and lush from early spring to late fall. Some of our other crops are oats, rye, rape, popcorn, blackeyed peas, tomatoes, sunflowers and cotton.

The yucca or soapweed, abundant in our pastures, blooms in late May, these blooms appear on a tall stem and are white lily-like flowers (the yucca tended to be a staple in the lives of the Plains Indian. It was used in the weaving of baskets and mats, the seeds were eaten, and the roots used both medicinally and as soap). Indian blanket, a low growing, brilliant orange, daisy-like flower is one of the most popular of all native wild flowers in our area. The purple blooms you see on rocky sites are probably loco weed (crazy weed). Mustard is blooming yellow and some in blue. Also from the mustard family is the western wallflower (yellow phlox or prairie rocket) which also blooms yellow.

The sandhill plum displays its snowy white blossoms in mid-April to early May before its leaves appear. These much resemble fruit blossoms such as apple, peach and pear. The plum thickets can be seen growing in pastures in low sandy areas.

The silver gray shrub you see abundant in the pastures is sage brush. It is native to Meade County, growing on sandy range land.

If you travel through in the summer months...

We harvest our wheat in mid-June right after it turns to a golden mature state and the kernels of wheat are dry enough to harvest and store. You will see much activity as the combines cut and thresh the grain and the trucks haul it to the elevators (those giant, white castles that dot our landscape).

Our corn, milo, and soybeans have been planted and are coming up in early summer. Most of these crops will be seen on irrigated farm ground in the perfect rows created by furrowing equipment to make a pathway for the irrigation water. Another form of irrigation is the sprinkler which creates a round field watered from gigantic water systems passing over the crops.

In late summer you might see a field of sunflowers following the sun with their beautiful heads.

Of the summer wild flowers the most predominate is the sunflower, the state flower of Kansas. These brilliant yellow flowers with their dark brown centers can be seen in just about every road ditch and pasture as far as the eye can see. You will also see the white bloom of the prickly poppy and the lavender "shaving brush" bloom of the wavy leaf thistle. The purple poppymallow or wine cup, grows on a low vine in road ditches and is a wine-colored beauty with gold anthers.

The sandhill plum ripens in July to early August. It is a native shrub and seldom grows above ten feet in height. The bright burgundy fruit it bears is a popular base for jelly and jam in our area made from recipes handed down from our pioneer grandmothers.

If you travel through in the Fall...

In the months of September or October, depending on the first frost, you can witness the harvest of our milo and corn crops. If the corn is cut for silage (feed for cattle) it is cut in the green stage, if for grain it is left until the stalks are brown and the corn is dry. The milo will present itself as fields of rusty brown heads growing about knee high. Milo is also used for feeding cattle. Soybeans and sunflowers are cut in October or November when the plants have completely dried out.

Our wheat, barley and oats are planted in early September and our alfalfa stays green through November.

As for wild flowers, you will still see sunflowers in the fall right up to the first frost. Goldenrod is another prevalent yellow flower, as is snake weed, a flower that grows boot-top high with dark green foliage and bright yellow flowers. It is said that snake weed blooms exactly 60 days before the first frost. The sand lily blooms white and can be seen until frost.

If you travel through in the winter...

About the only crop you see in the winter is the wheat which stays green all season given enough moisture.

The cows calve in February and March and you start to see mama and baby grazing on the green wheat.

January through March you can witness the migration of the tumble weed (Russian thistle) caught up in the cold Kansas winds. These thistles get ball-shaped from rolling across the ground, spreading their little seeds all over the country.

A few more facts...

One of the most prevalent trees you see along the road is the Siberian elm; these grow in pastures and along the creeks. The plains cottonwood is native to Meade County and grows along the roads and waterways. The little, gnarled trees seen in the pastures are most likely hackberry, we have two species: eastern and western. The Russian olive is not native to our area but is starting to spread from planted windbreaks and filling in low areas in our pastures. The vast windbreaks you see (trees obviously planted in straight rows to block the strong winter winds) were planted in the 40's and 50's as a conservation effort. These are mostly red cedar trees.

Drawings by Glen Feldman

Livestock raised in Meade County is mostly cattle, sheep and hogs. We have several feedlots in the county and two commercial dairy operations.

Wildlife in Meade County includes: porcupines, coyotes, foxes, raccoons, weasels, skunks, bobcats, white-tailed deer, jackrabbits, cottontails, fox squirrel, prairie dogs, striped ground squirrels, chipmunks, pocket gophers, rats, beavers, opossums, shrews, moles, bats, and an occasional armadillo.

We are a popular spot for the bird hunter in the fall with an abundant supply of ring-necked pheasant and bobwhite quail. Sixteen varieties of duck and three varieties of geese can also be found in Meade County, as well as wild turkey.

The windmills you see dotting the landscape are a very necessary implement to Meade County stock growers. We have very little live water here and have to pump it to the surface to water our livestock. Windmills are still sold in Meade as an economical way to pump water—one thing we can always count on is that Kansas wind!

It takes fifteen to twenty acres of pasture for one cow and her calf to survive for a year here, compared to four acres in eastern Kansas. Our pastures are mostly blue grama sometimes referred to as buffalo grass, a valuable forage plant for our livestock.

About every little town you pass by in Southwest Kansas has at least one grain elevator. These are the tall, white

castles along the railroad tracks where we store our grain. Most of our elevators are owned and operated by cooperatives made up of area farmers. The pickup is an indispensable vehicle to the farmer and will far outnumber the cars around local coffee shops on a rainy morning. Those long, white tanks on wheels you might have the misfortune to get caught behind on the highway are probably carrying anhydrous ammonia to fertilize the fields. Those low-flying airplanes swooping down back and forth across our farm ground could be spraying pesticides or herbicides on the crops to kill bugs or weeds that tend to put a dent in valuable yields.

As agriculture changes, so changes our county. You might pay particular attention to those beautiful old wooden barns and the occasional wooden windmill you see along the road; when they go they will be replaced by more efficient metal structures and lost forever with the homestead and covered wagon of our forefathers.

What you see along the road is but a small part of Meade County. If you are interested in history I urge you to stop in at the Meade County Historical Museum in Meade. If you like to camp, a trip to Meade State Lake south on K23 is well worth the drive. If you don't have time, just wave as you go along the road...and please...come again!

Meade State Lake and Park

by Nancy Ohnick

The Meade State Lake and Park is located twelve miles southwest of Meade on Highway K23.

Carved out of the Turkey Track Ranch in 1927, the Meade Lake is an oasis in the treeless grasslands of Southwest Kansas. It covers 443 acres and provides visitors with fishing, camping, and swimming opportunities. Boating is restricted to fishing boats, and campers can enjoy electrical hookups, a dumping station, bathhouse, and beach.

If I were to describe Meade Lake in one word, it would be *tranquil.* It's a great place to "get away from it all" for a weekend or vacation. The shady campgrounds surrounding the lake are well-kept and inviting. The camper who likes a peaceful surrounding will find Meade Lake a perfect place to camp.

A fisherman can find a number of challenging spots and can expect to catch catfish, bullhead, channel cat, bass, perch, and bluegill. There is a convenient boat ramp for putting your fishing boats in the water, as well as courtesy docks.

Wildlife enthusiasts and bird watchers will find the lake area a wonderful observation ground. There is a wildlife preserve west of the lake area providing great hiking and exploring as well as a nature trail with plant life identified. Considered by many the top spot in the central United States for bird watching, the lake area is inhabited by over 300 species. Spring migration usually hits late April, early May, with fall migration in mid-September.

Hunters often find the lake a great place to camp

during hunting season, and limited hunting is allowed in the wildlife area, but not at the lake.

The beach at Meade Lake is a great place to swim, build a sand castle, or just bask in the sun. There is a bath house with showers open in the summer months. Wind surfers can usually depend on a decent breeze to push them along.

When you visit Meade Lake, be sure to follow the signs to the Park Office and purchase the proper permits. More information may be obtained by writing to P.O. Box 1, Meade, KS 67864, or phoning (620) 873-2572.

A Brief History of Meade

Although Meade County was crossed by Coronado in his search for Quivira in 1541, written history of Meade County didn't begin until 1606, when England claimed the territory from the Atlantic to the Pacific. Exploration was also made by Spain beginning in 1528. France then claimed the area by exploration made from 1682 to 1724. After the United States made the Louisiana Purchase in 1803, France ceded their remaining territory to Spain. This area included Meade County. Mexico gained independence from Spain in 1821. Texas gained independence from Mexico in 1836, and was annexed to the United States in 1845. The State of Kansas was organized in 1854. In 1881, Meade County had been dissolved and made parts of Ford and Seward Counties, but was again established by an act of Legislature in 1885 with the present boundaries.

The American Indians, primarily Kiowa, Apache, Cheyenne, and Comanche, occupied the county before and after it was explored. The area was covered with a blanket of grass named for the buffalo which grazed millions of acres. The buffalo meant meat for the migrant tribes before the Indians were placed on reservations.

Meade was named after General George Gordon Meade, who led the Union Army of the Potomac during the Civil War.

The first settlement in what was to become Meade County was made in 1878. Many settlers came in 1884 through 1886 when the area was being promoted.

Meade Center had been started as a town on July 9, 1885, by the Meade Center Townsite Company, who had purchased 520 acres from the government. For this they paid $650. In the same year the original town site was surveyed, and by November, 1885, the city was incorporated and organized. The organization of Meade Center and the election of the first officers were legalized by an act of the legislature in 1889.

The name Meade Center was changed to Meade in 1889. The selection of Meade Center as county seat came only after several months of heated discussion and the official election on January 6, 1886.

Many street names came from real or "paper" towns which existed near the turn of the century in Meade County, such as Meade Center, Fowler, West Plains, Touszalin, Mertilla, Nirwana City, Atwater, Rainbelt, Red Bluff, Carmen, Roanoke, Byers, Artesia City, Uneda, Carthage, Helvetia, Belle Meade, Skidmore, Wilburn Spring Lake, Jasper and Jo-Ashe.

In 1887, the artesian wells in the valley north of Meade were discovered, and, with pure water, fertile soil, deposits of iron ore, peat, salt, silica, oil, and gas, the development of Meade County has progressed since that time.

Trails Across Meade County

The Adobe Walls Trail

This trail started near Adobe Walls, Texas, crossing Meade County about four miles south of Plains and going northeast about where the early towns of Jasper, Rainbelt, and Skidmore were, and then on to Dodge City.

The Bascom Trail

Known as the Fort Bascom Trail, it left the Jones and Plummer Trail near the Hoodoo Brown Road Ranch and turned southwest past the Big Springs Ranch and on toward Bascom, Texas, an old outpost in the Texas Panhandle. The soldiers of Fort Bascom gave protection from the Indians.

The Jones & Plummer Trail

The trail can still be seen north of Highway 54 to the west side of the CMS tower and can be seen from the air almost all the way to the

Oklahoma line. The first trail through the area was made by the Jones & Plummer Cattle Co., bringing their cattle from the Texas Panhandle on the Canadian River to Dodge City. As soon as Dodge City could handle freight, their company took teams of oxen and conestoga wagons and broke a trail through to the present site of Beaver, Oklahoma, then north to the Cimarron River, across Crooked Creek, and keeping to the high land to the east, came up the east edge of Meade before turning north, west of Fowler, and on to Dodge City.

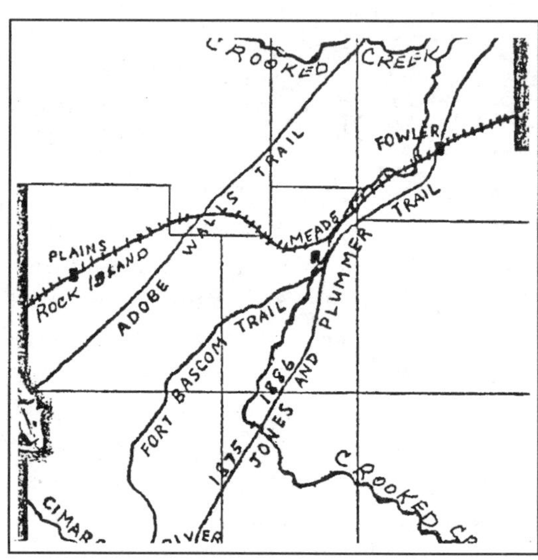

Hoodoo Brown Road Ranch on the Jones & Plumber Trail

Hoodoo Brown built a supply station made out of sod where flour, meat, soda, tobacco, sugar, and coffee could be purchased. There were also corrals for the freighters' stock, as well as hay and grain. At this time, Meade County was not organized. There was no post office, claim holder, or store in the entire county. In later years as the town of Meade was started, Hoodoo Brown gave the land which became Graceland Cemetery to Meade. The cemetery was named after his daughter, Grace, who was buried there.

Hoodoo must have been a friend to J.N. Whipple as a newspaper story in the Meade County Globe in 1886 reports: "Hoodoo Brown presented to J.N. Whipple the head of the buffalo killed by him last winter. Dr. Roberts preserved and mounted it and 'Whip' now has it over the door of his store as a reminder of what this country 'used to was'."

The Lone Tree Massacre

One of the last Indian battles in Kansas, The Lone Tree Massacre, occurred five miles southwest of Meade on the banks of Crooked Creek on August 24, 1874. Twenty-four Cheyenne from Fort Reno, Oklahoma, led by Chief Medicine Water, killed six members of a surveying team: Captain O.F.Short, one of his two sons, Truman Short, Mr. Shaw and his son, J.Allen, Harry Keuchler, and Harry C. Jones of Dodge City.

Two other surveying parties camped four miles south of Meade in the process of measuring township and range lines were unaffected. Soon after, the Indians were captured and sent to prison in Florida.

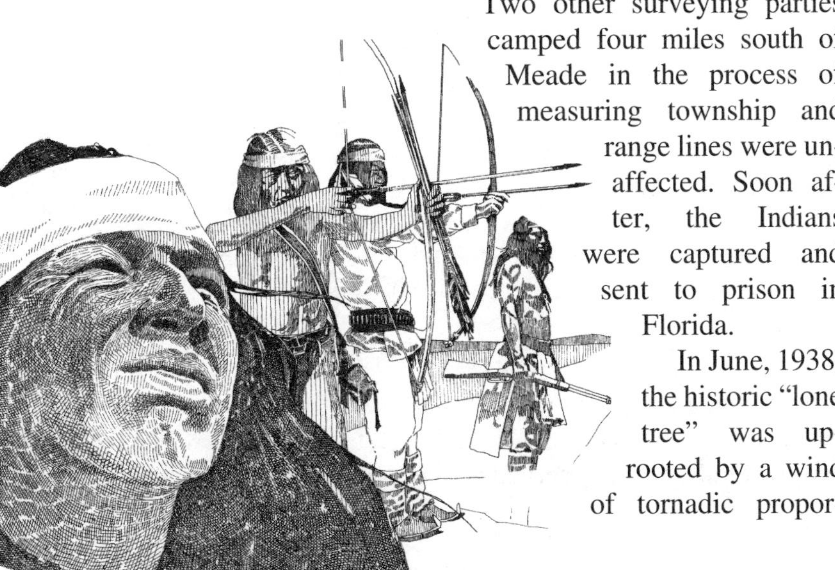

In June, 1938, the historic "lone tree" was uprooted by a wind of tornadic proportions. A portion of this tree can still be viewed at the Meade County Historical Museum.

Drawings by Glen Feldman

To learn more about Meade County history, we suggest: ***The Centennial History of Meade***, and ***Meade County History*** by the Meade County Historical Society. The Historical Society maintains an excellent museum, located at Carthage and Meade Center, dedicated to the people of Meade County and arranged in such a way as to depict their early lifestyle.